MALACHI DADS

The
HEART
of a
FATHER

MALACHI DADS

1 East Bode Road
Streamwood, IL 60107-6658 U.S.A.
awana.org
(630) 213-2000

3 4 5 17 16 15

KEY VERSE

... Choose this day whom you will serve ... But as for me and my house, we will serve the LORD.

—Joshua 24:15

LESSON 1 **MEMORY VERSE**

In the beginning, God created the heavens and the earth.

—Genesis 1:1

Lesson 1

CREATION

TOPIC 1 – GOD

God is the Creator of all things.

> *In the beginning, God created the heavens and the earth. The earth was without form and void, and darkness was over the face of the deep. And the Spirit of God was hovering over the face of the waters. —Genesis 1:1-2*

[Q] What's something you created that you're proud of?

The book of Genesis is the first book in the Bible, and it sets the stage for everything that follows in God's Word. Genesis describes the creation of everything — time, the universe, people, marriage, and so on. All of these things were created by God in the beginning.

Because God is the Creator of everything in the universe, He is also the Ruler of everything He created.

> *The LORD has established His throne in the heavens, and His kingdom rules over all. —Psalm 103:19*

[Q] What was your favorite sport or game to play when you were a kid? Why?

[Q] Why was it important to know the rules for that sport or game in order to succeed?

God sets the rules for how the world should work and what we are supposed to do as part of His creation. That means we need to understand the rules so that we can succeed in life — just like we would need to know the rules to succeed in any game or sport. That's why we have the Bible.

TOPIC 2 – PEOPLE

Human beings were created by God.

> *Then God said, "Let Us make man in Our image, after Our likeness. And let them have dominion over the fish of the sea and over the birds of the heavens and over the livestock and over all the earth and over every creeping thing that creeps on the earth." So God created man in His own image, in the image of God He created him; male and female He created them. —Genesis 1:26-27*

[Q] Why is it important for us to understand that God is our Creator?

[Q] What does it mean to be created in the image of God?

Not only were human beings created in the image of God, we were also created with a specific purpose: to worship God and bring Him glory. Look at the first lines of the Westminster Catechism:

Question: What is the chief end of man?

Answer: Man's chief end is to glorify God, and to enjoy Him forever.

[Q] What does it mean to be a religious person?

[Q] How would you describe what it means to worship something or someone?

Webster's Dictionary defines *worship* as: "showing devotion, reverence, love, veneration, admiration to someone or something." All people were created with a desire to worship God, which means even people who don't believe in God always end up worshiping something else.

DISCUSSING THE BIBLE

[Q] What have you learned about the Bible during this lesson?

[Q] Do you have any questions about what we've covered so far?

> *All Scripture is breathed out by God and profitable for teaching, for reproof, for correction, and for training in righteousness, that the man of God may be complete, equipped for every good work. —2 Timothy 3:16-17*

> *The law of the LORD is perfect, reviving the soul; the testimony of the LORD is sure, making wise the simple; the precepts of the LORD are right, rejoicing the heart; the commandment of the*

LORD is pure, enlightening the eyes; the fear of the LORD is clean, enduring forever; the rules of the LORD are true, and righteous altogether.
—Psalm 19:7-9

[Q] What did you like best about the verses we just read? Why?

[Q] How can the Bible help you become a "man of God"?

[Q] What do you need to do in order to make that happen?

DISCUSSING GOD

[Q] What have you learned about God during this lesson?

[Q] Do you have any questions about what we've covered so far?

Then the LORD God formed the man of dust from the ground and breathed into his nostrils the breath of life, and the man became a living creature. —Genesis 2:7

By faith we understand that the universe was created by the word of God, so that what is seen was not made out of things that are visible.
—Hebrews 11:3

[Q] What do you find interesting about the verses we just read? Why?

[Q] If you believe that God created everyone, how should that impact the way you treat other people?

[Q] How should that impact the way you think about yourself?

God is the Creator of all things, which means He is also the Ruler of all things — including all people.

> *Yours, O LORD, is the greatness and the power and the glory and the victory and the majesty, for all that is in the heavens and in the earth is Yours. Yours is the kingdom, O LORD, and You are exalted as head above all. —1 Chronicles 29:11*

[Q] Who is the main person in charge of these prison facilities?

[Q] What motivates you to obey that person? Why?

[Q] How is God similar to the person we just described? How is He different?

DISCUSSING PEOPLE

[Q] What have you learned about people during this lesson?

[Q] Do you have any questions about what we've covered so far?

> *Hear, O Israel: The LORD our God, the LORD is one. You shall love the LORD your God with all your heart and with all your soul and with all your might. —Deuteronomy 6:4-5*

> *But now, O LORD, You are our Father; we are the clay, and You are our potter; we are all the work of Your hand. —Isaiah 64:8*

[Q] What do you like best about the verses we just read? Why?

[Q] When have you tried to worship something or someone instead of God? How did it go?

[Q] What does it mean to worship God?

[Q] In what ways would you like your relationship with God to grow during this study? What will you need to do to help that happen?

Lesson 1

HOMEWORK

Complete the following assignments before the group gathers for Lesson 2.

Read Psalm 1:1-6 and answer the following questions:

1. What are the two choices (two paths) described in this psalm?

FOLLOW GOD. FOLLOW WICKEDNESS.

2. What are the consequences of following each choice?

PROSPER OR DESTRUCTION

Read Proverbs 1:1-33 and answer the following questions:

1. What is wisdom?

A TREASURE.

2. What are some benefits of seeking wisdom?

PEACE, DISCIPLINE, SUCCESS, KNOWLEDGE, DISCERNMENT

3. How do we gain wisdom?

SEEK GOD FEAR GOD TRUST GOD

4. What are the consequences of ignoring wisdom?

DESTRUCTION

Answer these questions about your life:

1. What is your main goal in life?

   FOLLOW JESUS. PRAISE JESUS.

2. What makes you happier than anything else?

   SERVING GOD, MY FAMILY, LIVING BY FAITH,

3. Who are the most important people in your life?

   AMBER, MADELYN, JACE, CLAY, CARL, RICK, SUZANNE.

4. Who are the people you most want to impress?

   SAME

5. Who or what have you been worshiping recently?

   WAS ME

6. How will you intentionally worship God this week?

   MORNING DEVOTION – SURRENDER, TRUST, HUMILITY, PRAY FOR, SERVE,

Review this week's memory verse:

> *In the beginning, God created the heavens and the earth. —Genesis 1:1*

LESSON 2 **MEMORY VERSE**

Keep your heart with all vigilance,
for from it flow the springs of life.

—Proverbs 4:23

Lesson 2

SIN

LESSON 1 REVIEW

Here are the key topics we covered during our last meeting:

- God is our Creator and Ruler.
- We can learn about God by looking at His creation.
- As our Creator, God has the right to set the rules for His creation.
- All people are created by God, and all people are created to worship Him.

LESSON 2 OBJECTIVES

Here are the key topics you'll be discussing in Lesson 2:

- Determine a definition for sin.
- Examine the cause and consequences of our sin.
- Identify Satan's strategy for attacking our weakness so that we will be ready when the attack comes.

GET TO KNOW GOD'S WORD

Opening question: Do you feel like you can trust the Bible? Why or why not? ABSOLUTELY – PERSONAL RELATIONSHIP.

- Time is one of the factors scholars use to decide whether an ancient book is reliable. Specifically, they look at the amount of time between the date a book was first written and the date of the oldest copy found. For example, if a book was written in A.D. 500 and the oldest copy available today was made in A.D. 1500, the difference would be 1,000 years.
- Here are the times between the original manuscript and the oldest available copy for a few famous authors that most people consider reliable:
    - Aristotle: 1,400 years
    - Caesar: 1,000 years
    - Plato: 1,200 years
- The amount of time between the original books of the New Testament and the earliest copies we have today is between 25-50 years.
- Conclusion: The Bible is the most reliable ancient book ever written, and we can be confident about what it says.

MAIN TOPIC 1 – SIN

[Q] What is sin, and where did it come from?

The Bible is the best place to find answers for life's biggest questions — including sin.

In order to understand sin, we need to understand that everything God created was good in the beginning:

> *And God saw everything that He had made, and behold, it was very good. And there was evening and there was morning, the sixth day.*
> *—Genesis 1:31*

[Q] What would paradise look like for you? Why?

When God created Adam and Eve, the first people, He placed them in a perfect place called the garden of Eden. Adam and Eve had everything they needed — food, fun, easy work, purpose and so on. Best of all, they often spent time in God's presence.

God only had one rule for Adam and Eve in paradise:

> *The LORD God took the man and put him in the garden of Eden to work it and keep it. And the LORD God commanded the man, saying, "You may surely eat of every tree of the garden, but of the tree of the knowledge of good and evil you shall not eat, for in the day that you eat of it you shall surely die." —Genesis 2:15-17*

[Q] Do you think this rule was fair? Explain.

Satan tempted Adam and Eve to sin by disobeying God. His main attack was to convince Adam and Eve that God couldn't be trusted:

> *... He* [Satan] *said to the woman, "Did God actually say, 'You shall not eat of any tree in the garden'?" And the woman said to the serpent, "We may eat of the fruit of the trees in the*

garden, but God said, 'You shall not eat of the fruit of the tree that is in the midst of the garden, neither shall you touch it, lest you die.'" But the serpent said to the woman, "You will not surely die. For God knows that when you eat of it your eyes will be opened, and you will be like God, knowing good and evil." So when the woman saw that the tree was good for food, and that it was a delight to the eyes, and that the tree was to be desired to make one wise, she took of its fruit and ate, and she also gave some to her husband who was with her, and he ate. —Genesis 3:1-6

[Q] How did Satan get Adam and Eve to doubt God's goodness?

[Q] What were some of the reasons why Adam and Eve chose to disobey God?

Adam and Eve's decision to sin brought consequences into their lives — and into the whole world.

To the woman He [God] *said, "I will surely multiply your pain in childbearing; in pain you shall bring forth children. Your desire shall be for your husband, and he shall rule over you." And to Adam He said, "Because you have listened to the voice of your wife and have eaten of the tree of which I commanded you, 'You shall not eat of it,' cursed is the ground because of you; in pain you shall eat of it all the days of your life; thorns and thistles it shall bring forth for you; and you shall eat the plants of the field. By the sweat of your*

face you shall eat bread, till you return to the ground, for out of it you were taken; for you are dust, and to dust you shall return."
—Genesis 3:16-19

[Q] Where do you see the consequences of sin in the world today?

[Q] How have you experienced the consequences of sin in your own life? AMEN - LIVING IT AT THIS MOMENT

Adam and Eve were perfect, but they still sinned against God and experienced major consequences — including physical death. The same has been true for every other person throughout the history of the world.

REVIEW

[Q] What did you learn from this week's homework? What questions would you like to ask?

[Q] How has what you learned helped you understand God better?

[Q] How has what you learned helped you understand yourself better?

Recite the memory verse from Lesson 1:

In the beginning, God created the heavens and the earth. —Genesis 1:1.

DISCUSSING THE BIBLE

[Q] What have you learned about the Bible during this lesson?

[Q] Do you have any questions about any of the verses we've covered so far?

DISCUSSING SIN

[Q] What is sin? Work together as a group to come up with a definition.

[Q] What does it mean to be tempted by something?

[Q] How does temptation push us toward sin?

Read the following passages and try to identify what they teach about the nature of temptation.

> *So when the woman saw that the tree was good for food, and that it was a delight to the eyes, and that the tree was to be desired to make one wise, she took of its fruit and ate, and she also gave some to her husband who was with her, and he ate. —Genesis 3:6*
>
> *Do not love the world or the things in the world. If anyone loves the world, the love of the Father is not in him. For all that is in the world —* ***the desires of the flesh and the desires of the eyes and pride of life*** *— is not from the Father but is from the world. —1 John 2:15-16* (emphasis added)

[Q] How did Adam and Eve experience the following aspects of temptation?

- The desires of the flesh
- The desires of the eyes
- The pride of life

[Q] What are some ways we experience these kinds of temptations today?

[Q] Who or what is Satan?

> *You are of your father the devil, and your will is to do your father's desires. He was a murderer from the beginning, and does not stand in the truth, because there is no truth in him. When he lies, he speaks out of his own character, for he is a liar and the father of lies. —John 8:44*

> *Be sober-minded; be watchful. Your adversary the devil prowls around like a roaring lion, seeking someone to devour. Resist him, firm in your faith, knowing that the same kinds of suffering are being experienced by your brotherhood throughout the world. —1 Peter 5:8-9*

[Q] What do these verses teach us about Satan?

[Q] How is Satan different from God?

[Q] Read Genesis 3:14-19 as a group. What were some of the physical consequences of the first sin?

[Q] What were some of the spiritual consequences?

[Q] How do see these consequences impacting the world today?

[Q] How do we know what God wants us to do each day?

[Q] If we're tempted to do something, how can we know whether it's right or wrong?

[Q] Where can we get help if we're unsure about something, or if we feel tempted and don't want to sin?

THE MALACHI DADS PLEDGE

As a Malachi Dad, I solemnly pledge to glorify God and build His kingdom by prioritizing the raising of godly children, first in my family, then in the influencing of other men to do the same in theirs. I firmly believe that my transformed life in Christ — my life of integrity, pursuit of this vision, and the pursuit of godly character — will allow me to impact my children, family and others towards this end.

I will practice a life of daily discipline and dependence on God through prayer and the study of God's Word for the wisdom in how to "nurture my children in the admonition of the Lord." I will pursue this endeavor for a lifetime whether my children are in my home or not.

Finally, I believe that my end goal is not only for my children to walk in the Lord but this God-given vision would impact multiple generations to come.

So help me God.

Lesson 2

HOMEWORK

Complete the following assignments before the group gathers for Lesson 3.

Read Genesis 39:7-12 and answer the following questions:

1. How did Joseph experience temptation?

   POTIPHARS WIFE.

2. How did Joseph respond to temptation?

   HE FOUGHT IT 100%.

Read 2 Samuel 11:1-4 and answer the following questions:

1. How did David experience temptation?

   BATHSHEBA

2. How did David respond to temptation?

   REBELLED, DENIED, COVERED

Use the following questions to compare and contrast these two Bible stories.

1. What were the similarities between Joseph's and David's temptations?

   SEXUAL LUST

2. What were the differences between their experiences?

Joseph resisted, David gave in.

3. What can you apply in your life from their examples?

I focus on Joseph

THE MALACHI DADS PLEDGE

As a Malachi Dad, I solemnly pledge to glorify God and build His kingdom by prioritizing the raising of godly children, first in my family, then in the influencing of other men to do the same in theirs. I firmly believe that my transformed life in Christ — my life of integrity, pursuit of this vision, and the pursuit of godly character — will allow me to impact my children, family and others towards this end.

I will practice a life of daily discipline and dependence on God through prayer and the study of God's Word for the wisdom in how to "nurture my children in the admonition of the Lord." I will pursue this endeavor for a lifetime whether my children are in my home or not.

Finally, I believe that my end goal is not only for my children to walk in the Lord but this God-given vision would impact multiple generations to come.

So help me God.

Review last week's memory verse:

> *In the beginning, God created the heavens and the earth. —Genesis 1:1*

Review this week's memory verse:

Keep your heart with all vigilance, for from it flow the springs of life. —Proverbs 4:23

LESSON 3 **MEMORY VERSE**

For God so loved the world,
that He gave His only Son,
that whoever believes in Him
should not perish
but have eternal life.

—John 3:16

Lesson 3

SALVATION

LESSON 2 REVIEW

Here are the key topics we covered during our last meeting:

- Adam and Eve were created in God's image. They were perfect, and they lived in a perfect paradise called the garden of Eden.
- Satan tempted Adam and Eve to sin by disbelieving God and disobeying Him.
- Adam and Eve chose to sin.
- The first sin had terrible consequences for Adam, Eve, the world and everyone in history.
- Each day we are given the same choice as Adam and Eve — to trust and obey God or to trust and obey Satan (and ourselves).

LESSON 3 KEY TOPICS

Here are the key topics for discussion this week:

- All people sin, which means all people are disqualified from eternal life with God.

- God chose to pay the penalty for our sin.
- God offers salvation to all sinners.

GET TO KNOW GOD'S WORD

Opening question: How well do you think people in our country today understand the Constitution? Explain your answer.

- The Bible was written by approximately 40 men. These men were from all walks of life: kings, peasants, fishermen, physicians, statesmen, scholars, poets and farmers. Each of these men was inspired by God through the Holy Spirit, but they wrote one or more books of the Bible in their own styles and personalities.
- The first parts of the Bible were written before 1500 B.C., and the last books were written around A.D. 100. That means the Bible was written over a period of more than 1,600 years.
- Even though the Bible was written by about 40 men who lived during a 1,600 year time period, the text of God's Word is consistent throughout. Everything fits together and communicates the same message about God, people, sin and salvation.
    - This is remarkable given that the Constitution was written by a group of men who lived during the same time period less than 250 years ago.
    - The Bible remained consistent because it ultimately came from God.
- Conclusion: The Bible is trustworthy and reliable.

MAIN TOPIC – SALVATION

[Q] When did you break something valuable as a kid? What happened next?

We've seen how Adam and Eve chose to sin against God, and we've said that their sin had terrible consequences for them, for the world, and for every other person who's ever lived. But what do those consequences mean for us?

Let's get a damage report for sin, starting with our condition as human beings after the fall:

> *The LORD saw that the wickedness of man was great in the earth, and that every intention of the thoughts of his heart was only evil continually. And the LORD regretted that He had made man on the earth, and it grieved Him to His heart. —Genesis 6:5-6*

> *God looks down from heaven on the children of man to see if there are any who understand, who seek after God. They have all fallen away; together they have become corrupt; there is none who does good, not even one. —Psalm 53:2-3*

[Q] What do these verses teach about people in general?

[Q] What do these verses teach about you specifically?

Now let's get a damage report about the consequences of our sin:

> *And you were dead in the trespasses and sins in which you once walked, following the course of this world, following the prince of the power of*

the air, the spirit that is now at work in the sons of disobedience. —Ephesians 2:1-2

For all have sinned and fall short of the glory of God, and are justified by His grace as a gift, through the redemption that is in Christ Jesus. —Romans 3:23-24

[Q] What do these verses teach about sin?

[Q] What do these verses teach about salvation?

All people sin, which means all people experience death — both physical death and spiritual death. Physical death is when our bodies stop working. Spiritual death is when we are separated from God for eternity.

Every person who sins becomes broken, with no ability to fix themself.

The good news is that God has chosen to fix us through His power. God offers us salvation through the death and resurrection of Jesus Christ.

For while we were still weak, at the right time Christ died for the ungodly. For one will scarcely die for a righteous person — though perhaps for a good person one would dare even to die — but God shows His love for us in that while we were still sinners, Christ died for us. —Romans 5:6-8

For the wages of sin is death, but the free gift of God is eternal life in Christ Jesus our Lord. —Romans 6:23

Because, if you confess with your mouth that Jesus is Lord and believe in your heart that God raised Him from the dead, you will be saved. For with the heart one believes and is justified, and with the mouth one confesses and is saved.
—Romans 10:9-10

[Q] What do these verses teach about the need for salvation?

[Q] What do these verses teach about the process of salvation — how it happens?

Salvation begins with the forgiveness of sin. When we confess our sinfulness to God and ask Him to save us (to fix what we've broken), He forgives our sin so that we are clean. But that's not all — our sin still has consequences.

For that reason, salvation also means that God took the penalty for our sin. The wages of sin is death, which is why Jesus chose to die on the cross for our sins.

[Q] What are the consequences of salvation? What happens to us when we are saved?

REVIEW

[Q] What did you learn from this week's homework? What questions would you like to ask?

[Q] How has what you learned helped you understand God better?

[Q] How has what you learned helped you understand yourself better?

Recite the memory verse from Lesson 2:

> *Keep your heart with all vigilance, for from it flow the springs of life. —Proverbs 4:23*

DISCUSSING THE BIBLE

[Q] What have you learned about the Bible during this lesson?

[Q] Do you have any questions about any of the verses we've covered so far?

DISCUSSING SALVATION

[Q] How would you describe salvation in a single sentence? Work as a group to come up with a working definition.

Read the following verses:

> *Because, if you confess with your mouth that Jesus is Lord and believe in your heart that God raised Him from the dead, you will be saved. For with the heart one believes and is justified, and with the mouth one confesses and is saved. —Romans 10:9-10*

> *And they said, "Believe in the Lord Jesus, and you will be saved ..." —Acts 16:31*

[Q] What does it mean to believe?

DISCUSSING THE TRINITY

The Trinity is our way of describing the different persons (or aspects) of God: God the Father, God the Son, and God the Holy Spirit. All three of God's aspects are involved in salvation.

First, God the Father is the ultimate source of salvation and the one who calls us to Himself. It is the Father who sent His Son and His Spirit to make a way for us to be saved.

> *But when the fullness of time had come, God sent forth His Son, born of woman, born under the law, to redeem those who were under the law, so that we might receive adoption as sons. And because you are sons, God has sent the Spirit of His Son into our hearts, crying, "Abba! Father!" —Galatians 4:4-6*

> *No one can come to Me unless the Father who sent Me draws him. And I will raise him up on the last day. —John 6:44*

[Q] What ideas or images come to mind when you hear the word *father*? Why?

[Q] How have you experienced God as your heavenly Father?

God the Son, whom we know as Jesus Christ, died on the cross to pay the penalty for our sins, because the wages of sin is death (Romans 3:23). Christ paved the way for our forgiveness and salvation when He rose from the dead, breaking the power of sin and death.

Christ is both the source of our righteousness and our Lord — our Master.

> *Jesus said to him, "I am the way, and the truth, and the life. No one comes to the Father except through Me." —John 14:6*

[Q] How do you react to the previous verse? Why?

> *Grace to you and peace from God our Father and the Lord Jesus Christ, who gave Himself for our sins to deliver us from the present evil age, according to the will of our God and Father. —Galatians 1:3-4*

> *He has delivered us from the domain of darkness and transferred us to the kingdom of His beloved Son, in whom we have redemption, the forgiveness of sins. —Colossians 1:13-14*

[Q] When have you experienced forgiveness from other people?

[Q] What does it mean to have our sins forgiven by God?

God the Holy Spirit teaches us about salvation through God's Word, the Bible. The Spirit seals our salvation — a process known as justification. The Spirit also lives inside of us and enables us to respond to God in faith and grow on a spiritual level, which is called sanctification.

> *And I will give you a new heart, and a new spirit I will put within you. And I will remove the heart of stone from your flesh and give you a heart of flesh. And I will put My Spirit within you, and*

cause you to walk in My statutes and be careful to obey My rules. —Ezekiel 36:26-27

When the Spirit of truth comes, He will guide you into all the truth, for He will not speak on His own authority, but whatever He hears He will speak, and He will declare to you the things that are to come. He will glorify Me, for He will take what is Mine and declare it to you. —John 16:13-14

In Him you also, when you heard the word of truth, the gospel of your salvation, and believed in Him, were sealed with the promised Holy Spirit, who is the guarantee of our inheritance until we acquire possession of it, to the praise of His glory. —Ephesians 1:13-14

[Q] In what ways have you encountered or experienced the Holy Spirit?

[Q] How would you define justification in your own words?

[Q] How would you define sanctification in your own words?

Here is a summary of what salvation is all about:

- Salvation is God's plan.
- As people, we are sinful and unable to save ourselves. That's why God paid the price for our sin.
- God offers salvation to all sinners.
- Each person of the Trinity is involved in salvation.
- People must believe (trust in Christ) in order to be saved.

[Q] What else would you like to know or learn about salvation?

PRAYER OF SALVATION

Dear God in heaven, I come to you in the name of Jesus. I acknowledge to You that I am a sinner and I am sorry for my sins and the life that I have lived. I need your forgiveness.

I believe that your only begotten Son, Jesus Christ, shed His precious blood on the cross at Calvary and died for my sins.

You said in Your holy Word, in Romans 10:9, that if we confess the Lord Jesus and believe in our hearts that God raised Him from the dead, we shall be saved.

Right now I confess Jesus as Savior. With my heart, I believe that God raised Jesus from the dead. This very moment I accept Jesus Christ as my own personal Savior and according to His Word, right now I am saved.

Thank you Jesus for Your unlimited grace which has saved me from my sins. I thank You, Jesus, that Your grace never leads to license, but rather it always leads to repentance. Therefore, Lord Jesus, transform my life so that I may bring glory and honor to You alone and not to myself.

Thank you Jesus for dying for me and giving me eternal life. Amen.

Name: ______________________________________ Date:________

Lesson 3

HOMEWORK

Complete the following assignments before the group gathers for Lesson 4.

Study the story of the rich young man in Matthew 19:16-26, then answer the following questions:

1. What do these verses teach about being saved?

2. What did the rich young man do right?

3. What did he do wrong?

4. How are you similar to the rich young man?

Read Acts 8:26-40, then answer the following questions:

1. What do these verses teach about being saved?

2. What did the Ethiopian eunuch do right?

3. How are you similar to the Ethiopian eunuch? How are you different?

4. Do you consider yourself to be saved? Explain why or why not in the space below.

Review this week's memory verse:

> *For God so loved the world, that He gave His only Son, that whoever believes in Him should not perish but have eternal life. —John 3:16*

LESSON 4 **MEMORY VERSE**

Sanctify them in the truth;
Your word is truth.

—John 17:17

Lesson 4

SANCTIFICATION

LESSON 3 REVIEW

Here are the key topics we covered during our last meeting:

- Salvation is God's plan. People are sinful and unable to save themselves.
- God paid the price for our sin.
- God offers salvation to all sinners.
- Each person of the Trinity is involved in salvation.
- Those who are saved must believe (put their trust) in Jesus Christ for their salvation.

LESSON 4 KEY TOPICS

Here are the key topics for discussion this week:

- God is holy and desires His followers to be holy.
- God works to produce Christlikeness (or holiness) in the believer.
- Sanctification is the process of becoming more like Christ.
- God's process for sanctification involves putting off old habits, renewing our minds, and putting on new habits.

GET TO KNOW GOD'S WORD

Opening question: Do you think it's possible for people to predict the future? Explain.

- There are places in the Bible where God told people what would happen in the future — this is called prophecy. Many of God's prophecies have already taken place, but some are still in the future.
- Here are some of the biblical prophecies that have already been fulfilled:
  - God spoke through the prophet Jeremiah to prophesy that the people of Jerusalem would be captives in Babylon for 70 years (see Jeremiah 25:11-12). It happened.
  - God spoke through the prophet Amos to prophesy that the nation of Israel would be reestablished after being destroyed (see Amos 9:14-15). It happened in 1948.
  - Several aspects of Jesus' life were prophesied in the Old Testament, including His birth in Bethlehem, His mother being a virgin, His betrayal for 30 pieces of silver, His death, His resurrection and many more.
- Conclusion: The prophecies that have come true are one of the reasons we can trust the Bible as a supernatural book — something that comes from God.

MAIN TOPIC – SANCTIFICATION

[Q] What's something good that you recently experienced for the first time?

When we become saved, we get to experience many new things through God and His Holy Spirit. For example, we get to experience the forgiveness of our sins. We become clean in God's eyes.

> *"Come now, let us reason together, says the LORD: though your sins are like scarlet, they shall be as white as snow; though they are red like crimson, they shall become like wool." —Isaiah 1:18*

We also become part of God's kingdom when we're saved. We move from beings citizens in the kingdom of darkness to being members of God's heavenly kingdom, with Jesus as our Lord.

> *He has delivered us from the domain of darkness and transferred us to the kingdom of His beloved Son, in whom we have redemption, the forgiveness of sins. —Colossians 1:13-14*

More, when we experience salvation and become part of God's kingdom, we have the blessing of God's Spirit living inside of us to guide us, support us, encourage us, teach us and correct us when necessary.

> *Do you not know that you are God's temple and that God's Spirit dwells in you? —1 Corinthians 3:16*

Best of all, experiencing salvation means we are changed into something new ourselves. We are no longer the same people, chained by our sins and failures. God changes us into new creations, and He gives us the chance to grow into the kinds of people He created us to be.

> *Therefore, if anyone is in Christ, he is a new creation. The old has passed away; behold, the new has come. —2 Corinthians 5:17*

[Q] Which of the new things we just talked about from salvation make you feel excited? Why?

[Q] How have you been changed by your experiences with God?

One of the parts of salvation is called *justification*. This is when God forgives our sins and removes the penalty for all the things we've done wrong. But this is just the beginning.

[Q] How many of you know someone who was given parole or finished their term in prison, was set free, but then was back in prison just a few months later?

Removing our punishment for sin (the wages of sin is death) doesn't stop us from making the same mistakes or choosing to disobey God in new and worse ways. That's why God also gives us the chance to grow. He helps us become more like Jesus as we learn about Him and are sensitive to His Spirit each day.

REVIEW

[Q] What did you learn from this week's homework? What questions would you like to ask?

[Q] How has it helped you understand God better?

[Q] How has what you learned helped you understand yourself better?

Recite the memory verse from Lesson 3:

> *For God so loved the world, that He gave His only Son, that whoever believes in Him should not perish but have eternal life. —John 3:16*

DISCUSSING THE BIBLE

[Q] What have you learned about the Bible during this lesson?

[Q] How would you summarize what prophecy is and why it's important?

DISCUSSING SANCTIFICATION

[Q] What are some of your main goals in life right now?

God has specific plans for our lives as individual Christians, but He also has goals that He wants all Christians to strive for and achieve. For example, God wants us to become better versions of ourselves by becoming more like Jesus.

> *As obedient children, do not be conformed to the passions of your former ignorance, but as He who called you is holy, you also be holy in all your conduct. —1 Peter 1:14-15*

> *But the fruit of the Spirit is love, joy, peace, patience, kindness, goodness, faithfulness, gentleness, self-control; against such things there is no law. —Galatians 5:22-23*

[Q] In which of those areas would you like to grow the most? Why?

To be a Christian should be to live as a disciple of Jesus. That means He is our Master — we choose to follow Him by doing what He does and believing what He believes. It also means we should choose to act in a way that is worthy of His name.

For you know how, like a father with his children, we exhorted each one of you and encouraged you and charged you to walk in a manner worthy of God, who calls you into His own kingdom and glory. —1 Thessalonians 2:11-12

For at one time you were darkness, but now you are light in the Lord. Walk as children of light (for the fruit of light is found in all that is good and right and true), and try to discern what is pleasing to the Lord. —Ephesians 5:8-10

[Q] What obstacles often keep us from walking in the light?

[Q] What are some practical ways we can work to overcome those obstacles?

[Q] How can we help each other live in a way that's worthy of God's kingdom and Christ's name?

We need to understand that sanctification is a gradual process. As we live from day to day and year to year, we slowly become more and more like Jesus. Like we said before, the Holy Spirit is deeply involved in this process:

And we all, with unveiled face, beholding the glory of the Lord, are being transformed into the same image from one degree of glory to another. For this comes from the Lord who is the Spirit. —2 Corinthians 3:18

The Bible is another important tool. The more we read and give ourselves to God's Word, the more we'll grow as disciples of Jesus.

All Scripture is breathed out by God and profitable for teaching, for reproof, for correction, and for training in righteousness, that the man of God may be complete, equipped for every good work. —2 Timothy 3:16-17

[Q] How do you feel about your experiences with the Bible right now?

[Q] What steps can we take to help each other get the most out of our time in God's Word?

We have an important choice to make in our own sanctification. That's because we must choose to let God change us. We must submit to His Spirit and His Word, rather than choosing to make our own decisions and keep control of our lives.

> *I appeal to you therefore, brothers, by the mercies of God, to present your bodies as a living sacrifice, holy and acceptable to God, which is your spiritual worship. Do not be conformed to this world, but be transformed by the renewal of your mind, that by testing you may discern what is the will of God, what is good and acceptable and perfect. —Romans 12:1-2*

We also must choose each day to reject our old, sinful ways of doing things. Instead, we must choose to follow Christ by "putting on" the new person He's made us.

> *... Put off your old self, which belongs to your former manner of life and is corrupt through deceitful desires, and to be renewed in the spirit of your minds, and to put on the new self, created after the likeness of God in true righteousness and holiness. —Ephesians 4:22-24*

In summary:

- Believers are to become more like Jesus.
- God gave believers His Word and the Holy Spirit in order to sanctify us.
- Believers sin by ignoring either the Bible or the Holy Spirit.
- As believers are sanctified, we become a good witness to the world.

THE MALACHI DADS PLEDGE

As a Malachi Dad, I solemnly pledge to glorify God and build His kingdom by prioritizing the raising of godly children, first in my family, then in the influencing of other men to do the same in theirs. I firmly believe that my transformed life in Christ — my life of integrity, pursuit of this vision, and the pursuit of godly character — will allow me to impact my children, family, and others towards this end.

I will practice a life of daily discipline and dependence on God through prayer and the study of God's Word for the wisdom in how to "nurture my children in the admonition of the Lord." I will pursue this endeavor for a lifetime whether my children are in my home or not.

Finally, I believe that my end goal is not only for my children to walk in the Lord but this God-given vision would impact multiple generations to come.

So help me God.

Review the verses you learned in the previous lessons.

Lesson 1:

> *In the beginning, God created the heavens and the earth. —Genesis 1:1*

Lesson 2:

> *Keep your heart with all vigilance, for from it flow the springs of life. —Proverbs 4:23*

Lesson 3:

> *For God so loved the world, that He gave His only Son, that whoever believes in Him should not perish but have eternal life. —John 3:16*

HOMEWORK

Complete the following assignments before the group gathers for Lesson 5.

Read Romans 12:9-21, then answer the following questions.

1. What do you like best about these verses? Why?

2. What do you find most challenging about these verses? Why?

3. Where will you find help and support to live the kind of life described in these verses?

Read 1 Corinthians 10:13, then answer the following questions.

1. What's your initial reaction to this verse? Why?

2. When have you felt like temptations or troubles were more than you could bear?

3. How will your life change if you believe without a shadow of a doubt that this verse is true?

4. What is a next step you would like to take in order to become more like Jesus?

THE MALACHI DADS PLEDGE

As a Malachi Dad, I solemnly pledge to glorify God and build His kingdom by prioritizing the raising of godly children, first in my family, then in the influencing of other men to do the same in theirs. I firmly believe that my transformed life in Christ — my life of integrity, pursuit of this vision, and the pursuit of godly character — will allow me to impact my children, family, and others towards this end.

I will practice a life of daily discipline and dependence on God through prayer and the study of God's Word for the wisdom in how to "nurture my children in the admonition of the Lord." I will pursue this endeavor for a lifetime whether my children are in my home or not.

Finally, I believe that my end goal is not only for my children to walk in the Lord but this God-given vision would impact multiple generations to come.

So help me God.

Review the verses you learned in the previous lessons.

Lesson 1:

In the beginning, God created the heavens and the earth. —Genesis 1:1

Lesson 2:

Keep your heart with all vigilance, for from it flow the springs of life. —Proverbs 4:23

Lesson 3:

For God so loved the world, that He gave His only Son, that whoever believes in Him should not perish but have eternal life. —John 3:16

Review this week's memory verse:

Sanctify them in the truth; Your word is truth. —John 17:17

LESSON 5 **MEMORY VERSE**

To each is given the manifestation of the Spirit for the common good.

—1 Corinthians 12:7

Lesson 5

THE CHURCH

LESSON 4 REVIEW

Here are the key topics we covered during our last meeting:

- God is holy and desires His followers to be holy.
- God works to produce Christlikeness (holiness) in all believers.
- Sanctification is the process of increasing in holiness and becoming more like Christ.
- God's process has three parts: put off the old (sinful habits), be renewed (think biblically), and put on the new (godly habits).

LESSON 5 KEY TOPICS

Here are the key topics for discussion this week:

- Christ is the head of the Church, which is the body of all believers.
- The Holy Spirit empowers and motivates believers.
- Sanctification is accomplished within believers.
- The Church witnesses about the glory and grace of God in this world.

GET TO KNOW GOD'S WORD

Opening question: Is there any way to use science to test or prove what the Bible says?

- The Bible describes many cities, kingdoms and kings that were lost over the centuries — scientists used to have no record of them outside of God's Word. As a result, many believed that the people and events described in the Bible were myths.
- Around 1800, several European nations (France and England especially) began excavating sites of ancient civilizations in the Middle East, which is how the science of archaeology began.
- Over the past 200 years, archaeologists have found the location of many biblical cities and discovered the timelines of their kings. Scientists have also provided a glimpse into the daily life of people during Old Testament times as numerous ancient languages have been decoded and thousands of texts translated.
- Archaeology now relies heavily on the biblical text for clues to the location of ancient cities, the dates of kings and kingdoms, and the location and dates of significant battles.
- Conclusion: The science of archaeology confirms rather than disproves the statements of the Bible.

MAIN TOPIC – THE CHURCH

[Q] What ideas or images come to mind when you hear the word *church*? Why?

[Q] What's a one-sentence definition for the Church in today's world?

The Church is the collection of all Christians across the world. It is much more than a building or a group of believers in a single place. The church is also called the Body of Christ because the Bible makes it clear that Jesus is the Head (or Master) of the Church.

> *And He put all things under His feet and gave Him as head over all things to the church, which is His body, the fullness of Him who fills all in all. —Ephesians 1:22-23*

> *And He* [Jesus] *is before all things, and in Him all things hold together. And He is the head of the body, the church. He is the beginning, the firstborn from the dead, that in everything He might be preeminent. —Colossians 1:17-18*

[Q] How would you describe the goal or mission of the Church?

The Church has several roles to play on earth. First, the Church is called to find and train new followers of Jesus. This is often referred to as making disciples, and it is a work that all Christians are called to.

> *And Jesus came and said to them, "All authority in heaven and on earth has been given to Me. Go therefore and make disciples of all nations, baptizing them in the name of the Father and of the Son and of the Holy Spirit, teaching them to observe all that I have commanded you. And behold, I am with you always, to the end of the age." —Matthew 28:18-20*

Second, the Church exists to serve God and bring Him glory.

You yourselves like living stones are being built up as a spiritual house, to be a holy priesthood, to offer spiritual sacrifices acceptable to God through Jesus Christ. —1 Peter 2:5

So that through the church the manifold wisdom of God might now be made known to the rulers and authorities in the heavenly places. To Him be glory in the church and in Christ Jesus throughout all generations, forever and ever. Amen. —Ephesians 3:10, 21

[Q] What does it mean to serve God? What does that look like?

[Q] As Christians and members of the Church, how do we bring glory to God?

REVIEW

[Q] What did you learn from this week's homework? What questions would you like to ask?

[Q] How has what you learned helped you understand God better?

[Q] How has what you learned helped you understand yourself better?

Recite the memory verse from Lesson 4:

Sanctify them in the truth; Your word is truth. —John 17:17

Review the memory verses from previous weeks:

Lesson 1:

> *In the beginning, God created the heavens and the earth. —Genesis 1:1*

Lesson 2:

> *Keep your heart with all vigilance, for from it flow the springs of life. —Proverbs 4:23*

Lesson 3:

> *For God so loved the world, that He gave His only Son, that whoever believes in Him should not perish but have eternal life. —John 3:16*

Lesson 4:

> *Sanctify them in the truth; Your word is truth. —John 17:17*

DISCUSSING THE BIBLE

[Q] What have you learned about the Bible during this lesson?

[Q] What questions do you have about archaeology or the trustworthiness of God's Word?

DISCUSSING THE CHURCH

[Q] How do we become part of the Church?

[Q] What are we supposed to do as members of the Church?

Review: The mission of the Church has three parts:

1. To make disciples of Jesus
2. To serve God
3. To bring glory to God

[Q] Are you able to participate in those parts of the mission in your current situation? Explain.

One of the ways we participate in the Church's mission is to study and apply the Bible.

> *All Scripture is breathed out by God and profitable for teaching, for reproof, for correction, and for training in righteousness, that the man of God may be complete, equipped for every good work.*
> *—2 Timothy 3:16-17*

[Q] What steps have you taken recently to study and apply God's Word?

Another way we participate in the Church's mission is to work with other members of the Church to support and encourage one another.

> *Be kind to one another, tenderhearted, forgiving one another, as God in Christ forgave you.*
> *—Ephesians 4:32*

Let love be genuine. Abhor what is evil; hold fast to what is good. Love one another with brotherly affection. Outdo one another in showing honor. —Romans 12:9-10

[Q] What's your initial reaction to these commands? Why?

[Q] How can you obey these commands in your life right now?

Sometimes we must keep each other accountable in order to be truly helpful and loving.

If your brother sins against you, go and tell him his fault, between you and him alone. If he listens to you, you have gained your brother. But if he does not listen, take one or two others along with you, that every charge may be established by the evidence of two or three witnesses. If he refuses to listen to them, tell it to the church. And if he refuses to listen even to the church, let him be to you as a Gentile and a tax collector. —Matthew 18:15-17

In order to serve God and participate in the mission of the Church, we must allow the Holy Spirit to guide us. The Spirit gives us the power and wisdom we need to live as disciples of Jesus.

If you love Me, you will keep My commandments. And I will ask the Father, and He will give you another Helper, to be with you forever, even the Spirit of truth, whom the world cannot receive, because it neither sees Him nor knows Him. You know Him, for He dwells with you and will be in you. —John 14:15-17

The Holy Spirit teaches us about God and helps us understand His Word. The Spirit also convicts us of sin when we start to go in the wrong direction.

> *These things I have spoken to you while I am still with you. But the Helper, the Holy Spirit, whom the Father will send in My name, He will teach you all things and bring to your remembrance all that I have said to you. —John 14:25-26*

> *Nevertheless, I tell you the truth: it is to your advantage that I go away, for if I do not go away, the Helper will not come to you. But if I go, I will send Him to you. And when He comes, He will convict the world concerning sin and righteousness and judgment. —John 16:7-8*

[Q] How have you experienced the Holy Spirit?

[Q] What steps can we take to involve the Holy Spirit in this group and in our individual lives?

The Holy Spirit also gives us gifts that we can use in serving God as members of the Church.

> *And He gave the apostles, the prophets, the evangelists, the shepherds and teachers, to equip the saints for the work of ministry, for building up the body of Christ, until we all attain to the unity of the faith and of the knowledge of the Son of God, to mature manhood, to the measure of the stature of the fullness of Christ.—Ephesians 4:11-13*

Here is a list of the spiritual gifts people can receive as members of the Church: administration, apostle, discernment of spirits, exhortation, faith, giving, healing, interpretation of tongues, knowledge, leading, mercy, miracles, prophecy, service, teaching, tongues, wisdom.

[Q] What are some of the gifts you've been given? How has God blessed you with talents and abilities?

[Q] How can you use your gifts right now to serve God in the Church?

> *But as it is, God arranged the members in the body, each one of them, as He chose. If all were a single member, where would the body be? As it is, there are many parts, yet one body. The eye cannot say to the hand, "I have no need of you," nor again the head to the feet, "I have no need of you." On the contrary, the parts of the body that seem to be weaker are indispensable, and on those parts of the body that we think less honorable we bestow the greater honor, and our unpresentable parts are treated with greater modesty. —1 Corinthians 12:18-23*

Remember: You are an important part of the Church. You were created by God with many gifts, and you can use those gifts to do great things for His glory.

THE MALACHI DADS PLEDGE

As a Malachi Dad, I solemnly pledge to glorify God and build His kingdom by prioritizing the raising of godly children, first in my family, then in the influencing of other men to do the same in theirs. I firmly believe that my transformed life in Christ — my life of integrity, pursuit of this vision, and the pursuit of godly character — will allow me to impact my children, family, and others towards this end.

I will practice a life of daily discipline and dependence on God through prayer and the study of God's Word for the wisdom in how to "nurture my children in the admonition of the Lord." I will pursue this endeavor for a lifetime whether my children are in my home or not.

Finally, I believe that my end goal is not only for my children to walk in the Lord but this God-given vision would impact multiple generations to come.

So help me God.

Lesson 5

HOMEWORK

Complete the following assignments before the group gathers for Lesson 6.

Read Revelation 2, focusing on what Jesus said to the different churches (rather than all the symbolism). Answer the following questions:

1. What were some things the churches were doing well? (What did Jesus like?)

2. What were some things the churches were not doing well? (What did Jesus correct them about?)

3. What kinds of advice did Jesus give to these churches?

Read Revelation 3, focusing on what Jesus said to the different churches (rather than all the symbolism). Answer the following questions.

1. What were some things the churches were doing well? (What did Jesus like?)

2. What were some things the churches were not doing well? (What did Jesus correct them about?)

3. What kinds of advice did Jesus give to these churches?

4. How will Jesus' words help you participate in your church this week?

THE MALACHI DADS PLEDGE

As a Malachi Dad, I solemnly pledge to glorify God and build His kingdom by prioritizing the raising of godly children, first in my family, then in the influencing of other men to do the same in theirs. I firmly believe that my transformed life in Christ — my life of integrity, pursuit of this vision, and the pursuit of godly character — will allow me to impact my children, family and others towards this end.

I will practice a life of daily discipline and dependence on God through prayer and the study of God's Word for the wisdom in how to "nurture my children in the admonition of the Lord." I will pursue this endeavor for a lifetime whether my children are in my home or not.

Finally, I believe that my end goal is not only for my children to walk in the Lord but this God-given vision would impact multiple generations to come.

So help me God.

Review this week's memory verse:

> *To each is given the manifestation of the Spirit for the common good. —1 Corinthians 12:7*

LESSON 6 **MEMORY VERSE**

Therefore a man shall leave his father and his mother and hold fast to his wife, and they shall become one flesh.

—Genesis 2:24

Lesson 6

MARRIAGE (PART 1)

MAIN THEMES

Here are the main themes we're concentrating on throughout this study (Two Paths):

- Every day we decide to either obey God or disobey. (Will we honor God or honor self?)
- There are consequences to each path — blessing or curse, heaven or hell.

LESSON 5 REVIEW

Here are the key topics we covered during our last meeting:

- Christ is the head of the Church, which is the body of all believers.
- The Holy Spirit empowers and motivates believers; He gives us the ability to obey.
- Sanctification is accomplished within the believer.
- The Church witnesses (testifies) to the glory and power of God in this world.

LESSON 6 OBJECTIVES

Here are the key objectives for discussion this week:

- Identify the origin of marriage.
- Explore the problems sin caused for marriage.
- Understand the biblical reasons for marriage.

GET TO KNOW GOD'S WORD

Opening question: What are some of your favorite catchphrases?

- In recent centuries, the English language has adopted many expressions based on the Bible. These expressions entered the language during a time when more people read the Bible and were familiar with what it said.
- Here are some of the expressions or phrases found in the Bible that we still use today:
  - An eye for an eye (Leviticus 24:19-20)
  - By the skin of my teeth (Job 19:20)
  - Dust to dust (Genesis 3:19)
  - A drop in the bucket (Isaiah 40:15)
  - Sour grapes (Ezekiel 18:2)
  - To cast the first stone (John 8:7)
- Conclusion: The Bible is an important source for today's culture.

MAIN TOPIC – MARRIAGE (PART 1)

[Q] What do we learn about marriage from modern movies and TV shows?

[Q] What have you learned about marriage so far in your life?

As Christians, the first thing we need to understand about marriage is that the whole thing was God's idea.

> *Then God said, "Let Us make man in Our image, after Our likeness. And let them have dominion over the fish of the sea and over the birds of the heavens and over the livestock and over all the earth and over every creeping thing that creeps on the earth." So God created man in His own image, in the image of God He created him; male and female He created them.*
> *—Genesis 1:26-27*

Men and women were created in God's image. God created them to rule over and care for His earthly creation, and to do it together.

[Q] Why is it important that God created human beings as male and female?

> *Then the LORD God said, "It is not good that the man should be alone; I will make him a helper fit for him." And the rib that the LORD God had taken from the man He made into a woman and brought her to the man. Then the man said, "This at last is bone of my bones and flesh of my flesh; she shall be called Woman, because she was taken out of Man." Therefore a man shall leave his father and his mother and hold fast to his wife, and they*

shall become one flesh. And the man and his wife were both naked and were not ashamed.
—Genesis 2:18, 22-25

[Q] What do these verses teach about the institution of marriage?

[Q] Why is it important that Adam and Eve *were both naked and were not ashamed*?

God designed marriage exactly the way He wanted it. Marriage is the core part of the family, and families are the building blocks of society. It's through marriage and family that we're supposed to learn the values of God's kingdom and how to live as members of the Church.

When Satan deceived Adam and Eve in the garden of Eden, he wasn't just attacking their relationship with God. He was also attacking their relationship with each other. And the result of Adam and Eve's sin is that marriage today can be corrupted and damaged by sin.

THE MALACHI DADS PLEDGE

As a Malachi Dad, I solemnly pledge to glorify God and build His kingdom by prioritizing the raising of godly children, first in my family, then in the influencing of other men to do the same in theirs. I firmly believe that my transformed life in Christ — my life of integrity, pursuit of this vision, and the pursuit of godly character — will allow me to impact my children, family and others towards this end.

I will practice a life of daily discipline and dependence on God through prayer and the study of God's Word for the wisdom in how to "nurture my children in the admonition of the Lord." I will pursue this endeavor for a lifetime whether my children are in my home or not.

Finally, I believe that my end goal is not only for my children to walk in the Lord but this God-given vision would impact multiple generations to come.

So help me God.

[Q] What emotions do you experience when you read this pledge? Why?

[Q] Where can you find the wisdom and strength necessary to fulfill this pledge?

REVIEW

[Q] What did you learn from this week's homework? What questions would you like to ask?

[Q] How has what you learned helped you understand God better?

[Q] How has what you learned helped you understand yourself better?

Recite the memory verse from Lesson 5:

> *To each is given the manifestation of the Spirit for the common good. —1 Corinthians 12:7*

DISCUSSING THE BIBLE

[Q] What have you learned about the Bible during this lesson?

[Q] What questions do you have about what we've studied so far?

DISCUSSING MARRIAGE

One of the reasons God created marriage is because He knows that people need companionship and mutual support — it's not good for us to be alone (Genesis 2:18). That doesn't mean all people are supposed to be married, but marriage is one way we can find the community and encouragement we need.

[Q] How have you seen marriage provide encouragement and support to the people you know?

Raising children is another important purpose of marriage. God expects us to teach our children about Him and how to live as a disciple of Jesus.

> *Train up a child in the way he should go; even when he is old he will not depart from it. —Proverbs 22:6*

> *Did He not make them one, with a portion of the Spirit in their union? And what was the one God seeking? Godly offspring. So guard yourselves in your spirit, and let none of you be faithless to the wife of your youth. —Malachi 2:15*

[Q] What are some words you would use to describe your childhood?

[Q] What words would you use to describe your parents' marriage?

The Bible makes it clear that followers of Jesus should only choose to marry other Christians:

> *Do not be unequally yoked with unbelievers. For what partnership has righteousness with lawlessness? Or what fellowship has light with darkness? —2 Corinthians 6:14*

[Q] Why is it important for Christians to marry other Christians?

[Q] If a Christian has married someone who doesn't know Jesus, where can that person find hope?

God created the marriage covenant to be permanent. He intended for a husband and wife to join together in unity for the rest of their lives, and He expected them never to violate that covenant.

> *Therefore a man shall leave his father and his mother and hold fast to his wife, and they shall become one flesh. —Genesis 2:24*

> *... Because the LORD was witness between you and the wife of your youth, to whom you have been faithless, though she is your companion and your wife by covenant. —Malachi 2:14*

> *A wife is bound to her husband as long as he lives. But if her husband dies, she is free to be married to whom she wishes, only in the Lord. —1 Corinthians 7:39*

[Q] How do these verses compare with our culture's view of marriage?

Sin has damaged the marriages within our society. One of the biggest ways marriages have been corrupted is through divorce.

[Q] What ideas or images come to mind when you hear the word *divorce*? Why?

> *And Pharisees came up to Him and tested Him by asking, "Is it lawful to divorce one's wife for any cause?" He answered, "Have you not read that He who created them from the beginning made them male and female, and said, 'Therefore a man shall leave his father and his mother and hold fast to his wife, and the two shall become one flesh'? So they are no longer two but one flesh. What therefore God has joined together, let not man separate." They said to Him, "Why then did Moses command one to give a certificate of divorce and to send her away?" He said to them, "Because of your hardness of heart Moses allowed you to divorce your wives, but from the beginning it was not so. And I say to you: whoever divorces his wife, except for sexual immorality, and marries another, commits adultery." —Matthew 19:3-9*

Divorce was never part of God's plan for marriage. It is something that people have come up with because of sin and the choice to follow their own desires.

[Q] How have you been impacted by divorce?

[Q] Where can you find hope in terms of recovering from your negative experiences?

As Christians, we need to understand that marriage is under attack today in several ways:

- Our culture is attempting to change the definition of marriage away from what God intended. For example:
  - Marriage between a man and a man, or between a woman and a woman
  - Marriage between a group of people
  - Men and women choose to live together without getting married — they view marriage as unnecessary.
- Our culture is also attempting to change the purpose of marriage away from what God desires.
  - People get married today for financial reasons.
  - People focus only on the sexual relationship, or choose to reject God's plan and engage in sex outside of marriage.
- Our culture continues to push the idea that marriages can be ended for any reason through divorce.

[Q] Where do you see these attacks evident in modern society?

[Q] How have you experienced these attacks in your own life?

[Q] What are some practical steps you can take to make your experience with marriage more biblical?

Summary:

- Marriage was designed by God.

- Marriage is for the mutual benefit of husbands and wives.
- Marriage is intended to reflect and glorify God.

Lesson 6

HOMEWORK

Complete the following assignments before the group gathers for Lesson 7.

Read Genesis 2:18-25, then answer the following questions:

1. How would you summarize the main idea of these verses?

2. What are three things God teaches us in this passage?

   a.

   b.

   c.

3. How can you apply these verses in your life?

Read Malachi 2:13-16, then answer the following questions:

1. How would you summarize the main idea of these verses?

2. God views marriage as a covenant, or contract. How does that impact your view of what marriage is and what marriage means?

3. How can you apply these verses in your life?

Review this week's memory verse:

> *Therefore a man shall leave his father and his mother and hold fast to his wife, and they shall become one flesh. —Genesis 2:24*

LESSON 7 **MEMORY VERSE**

Husbands, love your wives,
as Christ loved the church
and gave Himself up for her.

—Ephesians 5:25

Lesson 7

MARRIAGE (PART 2)

LESSON 6 REVIEW

Here are the key topics we covered during our last meeting:

- Marriage was designed by God for the mutual benefit of husbands and wives.
- Sin brought conflict into marriage and caused damage in the family.
- Marriage is a legal contract in God's eyes.
- Marriage fulfills many purposes — companionship, support, raising godly children and more.
- Marriage is under attack in our culture today.

Review the Malachi Dads Pledge:

As a Malachi Dad, I solemnly pledge to glorify God and build His kingdom by prioritizing the raising of godly children first in my family, then in the influencing of other men to do the same in theirs. I firmly believe that my transformed life in Christ — my life of integrity, pursuit of this vision, and the pursuit of godly character — will allow me to impact my children, family and others towards this end.

I will practice a life of daily discipline and dependence on God through prayer and the study of God's Word for the wisdom in how to "nurture my children in the admonition of the Lord." I will pursue this endeavor for a lifetime whether my children are in my home or not.

Finally, I believe that my end goal is not only for my children to walk in the Lord but this God-given vision would impact multiple generations to come.

So help me God.

LESSON 7 OBJECTIVES

Here are the objectives for discussion this week:

- Explore what it means to be a godly husband.
- Review the husband's role in a godly marriage.

GET TO KNOW GOD'S WORD

Opening question: What's the last book you read, and why did you read it?

- People who are skeptical of the Bible often claim that Christians have made up the divine origins of God's Word. They even claim that the Bible says nothing about being inspired by God. This is not true.
- The Bible claims in several places to be divinely inspired (written by God through human personalities), including these verses:

> *Knowing this first of all, that no prophecy of Scripture comes from someone's own*

interpretation. For no prophecy was ever produced by the will of man, but men spoke from God as they were carried along by the Holy Spirit.
—2 Peter 1:20-21

All Scripture is breathed out by God and profitable for teaching, for reproof, for correction, and for training in righteousness. —2 Timothy 3:16

- Conclusion: The Bible claims to be a supernatural collection of books that is divinely inspired by God.

MAIN TOPIC – MARRIAGE (PART 2)

[Q] What does our culture teach us about sex?

[Q] What have you learned about sex from the church?

The first thing we need to understand about sex is that God created it as a gift to be enjoyed in the context of marriage. That was His plan for sex from the beginning.

Therefore a man shall leave his father and his mother and hold fast to his wife, and they shall become one flesh. And the man and his wife were both naked and were not ashamed.
—Genesis 2:24-25

Let marriage be held in honor among all, and let the marriage bed be undefiled, for God will judge the sexually immoral and adulterous. —Hebrews 13:4

But sexual immorality and all impurity or covetousness must not even be named among you, as is proper among saints. —Ephesians 5:3

[Q] How do you respond to those verses? Why?

God's plan for sex was for a man and a woman to enjoy themselves within the context of marriage. Any other kind of sexual activity goes against God's plan, which makes it sin.

> *For this is the will of God, your sanctification: that you abstain from sexual immorality; that each one of you know how to control his own body in holiness and honor, not in the passion of lust like the Gentiles who do not know God.*
> *—1 Thessalonians 4:3-5*

[Q] Why is it sometimes so difficult for us to control our bodies?

Sex isn't supposed to be a bullying point or a bargaining chip. Instead, when two people are married, they should give themselves to each other often, and they should give themselves as a gift. This kind of sexual intimacy pleases God.

> *But because of the temptation to sexual immorality, each man should have his own wife and each woman her own husband. The husband should give to his wife her conjugal rights, and likewise the wife to her husband. For the wife does not have authority over her own body, but the husband does. Likewise the husband does not have authority over his own body, but the wife does. Do not deprive one another, except perhaps by agreement for a limited time, that you may devote yourselves to prayer; but then come together again, so that Satan may not tempt you because of your lack of self-control. —1 Corinthians 7:2-5*

[Q] What do you know about sex now that you wish you knew when you were younger?

REVIEW

[Q] What did you learn from this week's homework? What questions would you like to ask?

[Q] How has what you learned helped you understand God better?

[Q] How has what you learned helped you understand yourself better?

Recite the memory verse from Lesson 6:

> *Therefore a man shall leave his father and his mother and hold fast to his wife, and they shall become one flesh.*
> *—Genesis 2:24*

DISCUSSING THE BIBLE

[Q] What have you learned about the Bible during this lesson?

[Q] How do you react to the fact that the Bible claims to be inspired by God?

DISCUSSING MARRIAGE AND SEX

[Q] Throughout your life, who taught you what it means to be a husband?

[Q] What did you learn most from those individuals?

As Christians, what we do in our families is vitally important. As husbands, we answer to God when it comes to the way we treat our wives and children.

> *But I want you to understand that the head of every man is Christ, the head of a wife is her husband, and the head of Christ is God.*
> *—1 Corinthians 11:3*

All husbands are leaders. God has called husbands to take a leadership role in their families, which includes supporting and sacrificing for their wives and children.

> *Wives, submit to your own husbands, as to the Lord. For the husband is the head of the wife even as Christ is the head of the church, His body, and is Himself its Savior.*
> *—Ephesians 5:22-23*

> *Husbands, love your wives, as Christ loved the church and gave Himself up for her.*
> *—Ephesians 5:25*

[Q] Do you consider yourself to be a leader? Explain.

[Q] What are some decisions that need to be made by the leader in a family?

God doesn't want husbands to just lead their wives. He also expects husbands to love their wives in a real and powerful way.

> *In the same way husbands should love their wives as their own bodies. He who loves his wife loves himself. For no one ever hated his own flesh, but nourishes and cherishes it, just as Christ does the church, because we are members of His body.*
> *—Ephesians 5:28-30*

> *Love is patient and kind; love does not envy or boast; it is not arrogant or rude. It does not insist on its own way; it is not irritable or resentful; it does not rejoice at wrongdoing, but rejoices with the truth. Love bears all things, believes all things, hopes all things, endures all things.*
> *—1 Corinthians 13:4-7*

> *Let your fountain be blessed, and rejoice in the wife of your youth, a lovely deer, a graceful doe. Let her breasts fill you at all times with delight; be intoxicated always in her love.*
> *—Proverbs 5:18-19*

[Q] How do you respond to those verses?

[Q] When have you experienced the kind of love described in 1 Corinthians 13?

[Q] What are some ways that Christ showed love to the Church?

Love and bitterness don't mix, which is why husbands are called to use love as a way of solving conflict and strife in the family. Remember that anyone can take from other people, but true leaders (and true lovers) are the ones who choose to give.

Husbands are leaders, husbands are lovers, and husbands are also learners. In order to love and lead your wife, you must learn who she is and what she needs.

> *Likewise, husbands, live with your wives in an understanding way, showing honor to the woman as the weaker vessel, since they are heirs with you of the grace of life, so that your prayers may not be hindered. —1 Peter 3:7*

[Q] What are some ways that a husband can learn about his wife?

Finally, husbands are called to be providers. We take care of our families, choosing to put their needs ahead of our own.

> *But if anyone does not provide for his relatives, and especially for members of his household, he has denied the faith and is worse than an unbeliever. —1 Timothy 5:8*

> *For even when we were with you, we would give you this command: If anyone is not willing to work, let him not eat. For we hear that some among you walk in idleness, not busy at work, but busybodies. Now such persons we command and encourage in the Lord Jesus Christ to do their work quietly and to earn their own living. —2 Thessalonians 3:10-12*

[Q] How do you respond to those verses? Why?

[Q] What steps can you take to improve as a provider for your family?

Lesson 7

HOMEWORK

Complete the following assignments before the group gathers for Lesson 8.

Read Ephesians 4:1-3, then answer the following questions.

1. How do these verses command Christians to behave? (What are we supposed to do?)

2. How do the commands in these verses apply to the roles of a husband?

3. In what ways can you improve at applying the commands in these verses?

Read these verses: Proverbs 10:12, 12:18, 13:10, 15:1, 16:21, 16:32, and 19:11. When you're finished, answer the following questions:

1. What are some common themes in these verses?

2. What are the benefits of wise speech?

3. What are the dangers of harsh speech?

4. How do these verses apply to your roles as a husband?

Review the verses you learned in the previous lessons.

Lesson 1:

> *In the beginning, God created the heavens and the earth. —Genesis 1:1*

Lesson 2:

> *Keep your heart with all vigilance, for from it flow the springs of life. —Proverbs 4:23*

Lesson 3:

> *For God so loved the world, that He gave His only Son, that whoever believes in Him should not perish but have eternal life. —John 3:16*

Lesson 4:

> *Sanctify them in the truth; Your word is truth. —John 17:17*

Lesson 5:

> *To each is given the manifestation of the Spirit for the common good. —1 Corinthians 12:7*

Lesson 6:

> *Therefore a man shall leave his father and his mother and hold fast to his wife, and they shall become one flesh. —Genesis 2:24*

Review this week's memory verse:

> *Husbands, love your wives, as Christ loved the church and gave Himself up for her.*
> *—Ephesians 5:25*

LESSON 8 **MEMORY VERSE**

In the fear of the LORD one has strong confidence, and his children will have a refuge.

—Proverbs 14:26

Lesson 8

FATHERING (PART 1)

KEY BELIEFS

Remember the key beliefs for this study:

- God is real, and He is in charge of all things.
- God's Word is true. God gave us the Bible for our benefit and guidance.
- The Bible is all we need to understand our world, and to live in a way that pleases God. Following the Bible allows us to help our families, neighbors, and country.

LESSON 7 REVIEW

Here are the key topics we covered during our last meeting:

- Marriage between a man and a woman is the only place for sex.
- Sex is a gift from God designed to be enjoyed, but not abused.
- Husbands are accountable to God for the way they treat their families.
- A husband is a leader, lover, learner, and provider.

LESSON 8 OBJECTIVES

Here are the key objectives for discussion this week:

- Clarify the relationship between fathers and children.
- Identify the characteristics of a godly family environment.
- Explore a warning to fathers.

GET TO KNOW GOD'S WORD

Opening question: What are some ways our culture has been influenced by the Bible?

- The Bible has been the foundation for many cultural changes throughout the centuries, including the Protestant Reformation.
- For many years, there was only one kind of Christian church in the world. This was a good thing and helped the church spread a unified message. Slowly, however, the church began to drift away from biblical teaching. The people in charge began to seek out corrupt practices and teach false doctrines.
- In 1517, a man named Martin Luther posted 95 discussion points on his local cathedral. These were 95 ways he felt the church was working against the Bible. This was the beginning of what we now call the Protestant Reformation. As a result of Luther's dedication to God's Word, the Protestant church was born. Churches around the world recommitted to teaching the truths of God's Word — that salvation is by faith alone, in Christ alone, on the authority of the Bible alone, and all to the glory of God.

MAIN TOPIC – FATHERING (PART 1)

[Q] What's the most important relationship within a family? Explain.

> *He* [Jesus] *answered, "Have you not read that He who created them from the beginning made them male and female, and said, 'Therefore a man shall leave his father and his mother and hold fast to his wife, and the two shall become one flesh?' So they are no longer two but one flesh. What therefore God has joined together, let not man separate." —Matthew 19:4-6*

> *When a man is newly married, he shall not go out with the army or be liable for any other public duty. He shall be free at home one year to be happy with his wife whom he has taken. —Deuteronomy 24:5*

The primary relationship in the family is the relationship between husband and wife. The husband/wife relationship is designed to be permanent, while most children leave their parents to start their own homes and families. The bond between a husband and wife even takes priority over national defense!

Unfortunately, our culture has the family priority reversed. Children are given priority over the parents in most families today; the activities and schedule revolve around the children, not the parents. As a result, parents become worn out and kids become self-centered and slow to mature.

[Q] What do movies and TV shows teach about the relationship between husband and wife?

[Q] What do they teach about the relationships between parents and kids?

When we keep the proper priorities in our homes, we can fully appreciate that children are a blessing given to us by God. Children bring us joy, but they also represent a responsibility. Parents are stewards charged to raise their children in a way that helps them worship and honor God from their youngest days.

> *Behold, children are a heritage from the LORD, the fruit of the womb a reward. Like arrows in the hand of a warrior are the children of one's youth. —Psalm 127:3-4*

> *Did He not make them one, with a portion of the Spirit in their union? And what was the one God seeking? Godly offspring. So guard yourselves in your spirit, and let none of you be faithless to the wife of your youth. —Malachi 2:15*

Summary:

- It is God who gives children to us.
- Parents are responsible to raise their children in a godly manner.
- Parenting is both an honor and a responsibility, both of which are given by God.

REVIEW

[Q] What did you learn from this week's homework? What questions would you like to ask?

[Q] How has what you learned helped you understand God better?

[Q] How has what you learned helped you understand yourself better?

Recite the memory verse from Lesson 7:

> *Husbands, love your wives, as Christ loved the church and gave Himself up for her.*
> *—Ephesians 5:25*

DISCUSSING THE BIBLE

[Q] What have you learned about the Bible during this lesson?

[Q] After almost two months in this study, what do you appreciate most about God's Word? Why?

DISCUSSING PARENTING

[Q] What ideas or images come to mind when you hear the word *fear*? Why?

The Bible teaches about several characteristics godly parents should have, but the fear of the Lord is one of the most important.

> *Blessed is everyone who fears the LORD, who walks in His ways! You shall eat the fruit of the labor of your hands; you shall be blessed, and it shall be well with you. Your wife will be like a fruitful vine within your house; your children will be like olive shoots around your table. Behold, thus shall the man be blessed who fears the LORD. —Psalm 128:1-4*

[Q] What do these verses teach about healthy families?

[Q] How would you define what it means to fear the Lord?

The fear of the Lord is a reverent awe of God that leads to a desire to obey, trust, and honor Him. This attitude is a gift of the Lord and leads to many blessings in our lives.

Let's look at some other characteristics of godly families. First, the home should be a place where all people feel respected — including Mom and Dad.

> *Honor your father and your mother, as the LORD your God commanded you, that your days may be long, and that it may go well with you in the land that the LORD your God is giving you.*
> *—Deuteronomy 5:16*

> *If one curses his father or his mother, his lamp will be put out in utter darkness. —Proverbs 20:20*

[Q] Was your home a place of respect when you were a child? Explain.

[Q] As parents, how can we know when our children respect us?

[Q] How can we help our children respect us?

Second, a godly home should be a place of safety and refuge. Fear, anger, and unforgiveness have no place in the home. Instead, all family members should look forward to being home. As fathers, we have a great opportunity to influence our home environments.

In the fear of the LORD one has strong confidence, and his children will have a refuge. —Proverbs 14:26

Children, obey your parents in the Lord, for this is right. "Honor your father and mother" (this is the first commandment with a promise), "that it may go well with you and that you may live long in the land." Fathers, do not provoke your children to anger, but bring them up in the discipline and instruction of the Lord. —Ephesians 6:1-4

[Q] What does it look like when family members don't feel safe within their homes? What happens in those situations?

[Q] What steps can we take as fathers to make sure our homes are places of safety and refuge?

Third, godly homes are places where people learn about God and learn how to experience His presence. They are places where children receive moral training and parents choose to do what is right. This is one of our main responsibilities as fathers.

And these words that I command you today shall be on your heart. You shall teach them diligently to your children, and shall talk of them when you sit in your house, and when you walk by the way, and when you lie down, and when you rise. You shall bind them as a sign on your hand, and they shall be as frontlets between your eyes. You shall write them on the doorposts of your house and on your gates. —Deuteronomy 6:6-8

[Q] What are the different types of situations described in these verses?

[Q] What do these situations look like in our lives today?

> *My son, keep your father's commandment, and forsake not your mother's teaching. Bind them on your heart always; tie them around your neck. When you walk, they will lead you; when you lie down, they will watch over you; and when you awake, they will talk with you. —Proverbs 6:20-23*

[Q] How can you teach your children about God in your current situation?

One of the worst things we can do as fathers (and husbands) is to lash out in anger. Wrath is something for God to demonstrate, not us. At the same time, we need to provide guidelines for our children to help them understand what God desires for them.

> *Husbands, love your wives, and do not be harsh with them. Children, obey your parents in everything, for this pleases the Lord. Fathers, do not provoke your children, lest they become discouraged. —Colossians 3:19-21*

> *Know this, my beloved brothers: let every person be quick to hear, slow to speak, slow to anger; for the anger of man does not produce the righteousness of God. —James 1:19-20*

> *The rod and reproof give wisdom, but a child left to himself brings shame to his mother.*
> *—Proverbs 29:15*

[Q] How would you describe your experiences with discipline as a child?

[Q] How do we discipline our children without lashing out in anger?

Summary:

· The relationship between husband and wife is primary in a family.

· A godly father must fear the Lord.

· Families are a place of respect, honor, safety and godly teaching.

· Fathers are warned not to provoke their children.

Lesson 8

HOMEWORK

Complete the following assignments before the group gathers for Lesson 9.

Make a list of everything you appreciate about each of your children. Be as specific as you can.

Is there any person in your family with whom you have difficulty communicating? Who?

- What can you do to remove barriers?
- What can you do to improve communication?

What are some ways you have provoked your children or lashed out in anger?

What steps can you take in the coming weeks to guide your children in a godly way?

Review this week's memory verse:

> *In the fear of the LORD one has strong confidence, and his children will have a refuge.*
> *—Proverbs 14:26*

HOMEWORK

LESSON 9 **MEMORY VERSE**

Train up a child in the way
he should go; even when he is old
he will not depart from it.

—Proverbs 22:6

Lesson 9

FATHERING (PART 2)

REVIEW

Remember our Two Paths theme for this study:

- Every day we decide to either obey God or disobey Him — to honor God or to honor ourselves.
- There are consequences to each path.

Here are the key topics we covered during our last meeting:

- Marriage is the primary human relationship — the connection between husband and wife.
- A godly husband and father must fear the Lord.
- A godly family environment is a place of respect, safety and teaching.
- Fathers should not provoke their children or lash out in anger.
- Fathers should raise children in the teaching and admonition of the Lord.

LESSON 9 OBJECTIVES

Here are the objectives for discussion this week:

- Define godly discipline.

- Consider how to apply godly discipline.
- Identify culturally unbiblical ways to raise children.
- Summarize biblical advice for stepfamilies.

GET TO KNOW GOD'S WORD

Opening question: What do you remember or admire about the United States Constitution?

- Many European settlers came to America in search of freedom — specifically religious freedom.
- The U.S. Constitution is based on a biblical view of man, government and justice.
- The foundation of the United States is based on Christian values.

MAIN TOPIC – FATHERING (PART 2)

[Q] What does our culture teach us about the relationship between fathers and their children?

We need to understand that God intended fathers to be one of the most significant relationships and influences in the lives of children, and He created children to naturally look up to their fathers. Children want to be proud of their dads and have to be convinced otherwise.

> *Grandchildren are the crown of the aged, and the glory of children is their fathers.* —Proverbs 17:6

Discipline is a natural part of the relationship between fathers and children. Even though they don't know it or appreciate it, godly discipline is one of the things kids need most from their dads.

The word *discipline* is often used negatively. Actually, discipline is meant to be a loving approach to teaching children appropriate behavior. It comes from the word *disciple* and literally means "to teach" or "to mold." Children need discipline to become healthy, mature adults.

> *"My son, do not regard lightly the discipline of the Lord, nor be weary when reproved by Him. For the Lord disciplines the one He loves, and chastises every son whom He receives." It is for discipline that you have to endure. God is treating you as sons. For what son is there whom his father does not discipline? If you are left without discipline, in which all have participated, then you are illegitimate children and not sons. Besides this, we have had earthly fathers who disciplined us and we respected them. Shall we not much more be subject to the Father of spirits and live? —Hebrews 12:5b-9*

[Q] How would you summarize the main message of these verses?

[Q] Where have you seen godly discipline done well?

I'm living it!

> *Train up a child in the way he should go; even when he is old he will not depart from it. —Proverbs 22:6*

[Q] What's your first reaction to this verse? Why?

Let's spend a few minutes reviewing some biblical tips for godly parenting:

- Children left to themselves will go in the wrong direction (Proverbs 29:15).
- If you allow children to go their own way, they will likely do so their whole life.
  - Proverbs 22:6 is advice, not a promise.
  - Even good parents can have bad children.
- Never discipline a child in uncontrolled anger, because wrath does not produce righteousness (James 1:19-20).
- Discipline with the goal of raising a child who is wise.
- Discipline is for changing behavior, not punishment — the goal is to develop godly habits.

[Q] What questions do you have about these biblical tips?

[Q] What other tips or themes from the Bible can help us discipline children in a godly way?

Let's finish this portion of the study by reviewing some practical tips for godly parenting:

- Never discipline in public. Kids will focus on the people watching, not the issue being corrected.
- Discipline children because they did wrong, not because they made you angry or embarrassed. (Be sure to hug and pray afterwards.)
- During and after discipline, be sure to explain what was wrong according to God's rules.

[Q] What questions do you have about these practical tips?

[Q] What other tips or ideas can help us discipline children in a godly way?

REVIEW

[Q] What did you learn from this week's homework? What questions would you like to ask?

[Q] How has what you learned helped you understand God better?

[Q] How has what you learned helped you understand yourself better?

Recite the memory verse from Lesson 8:

> *In the fear of the LORD one has strong confidence, and his children will have a refuge.*
> *—Proverbs 14:26*

DISCUSSING THE BIBLE

[Q] What have you learned about the Bible during this lesson?

[Q] After more than two months in this study, what are the main questions you would like answered about God's Word?

DISCUSSING FATHERING

[Q] What do you remember most fondly about your father growing up?

Lloyd

[Q] Looking back, in what areas did your father struggle as a parent?

Godly fathers are committed to disciplining their children.

> *And have you forgotten the exhortation that addresses you as sons? "My son, do not regard lightly the discipline of the Lord, nor be weary when reproved by Him. For the Lord disciplines the one He loves, and chastises every son whom He receives." —Hebrews 12:5-6*

[Q] How should the age of our children influence the decisions we make about discipline?

One type of discipline is reproof. This is any kind of verbal discipline, including instruction, encouragement, correction, warning, teaching, prayer, persuasion and more.

> *All Scripture is breathed out by God and profitable for teaching, for reproof, for correction, and for training in righteousness, that the man of God may be complete, equipped for every good work. —2 Timothy 3:16-17*

> *Whoever loves discipline loves knowledge, but he who hates reproof is stupid. —Proverbs 12:1*

[Q] How do you respond to these verses?

[Q] How does our culture teach parents to discipline their children?

Let's look at some more tips in the Bible for how to discipline children in a godly way. First, we should remember that anger usually doesn't help us achieve our goals as parents.

> *A soft answer turns away wrath, but a harsh word stirs up anger. The tongue of the wise commends knowledge, but the mouths of fools pour out folly.* —*Proverbs 15:1-2*

Second, we can help our cause as fathers by teaching our children about God, and by reminding our children of God's blessings in the past.

> *And he said to the people of Israel, "When your children ask their fathers in times to come, 'What do these stones mean?' then you shall let your children know, 'Israel passed over this Jordan on dry ground.' For the LORD your God dried up the waters of the Jordan for you until you passed over, as the LORD your God did to the Red Sea, which he dried up for us until we passed over, so that all the peoples of the earth may know that the hand of the LORD is mighty, that you may fear the LORD your God forever."* —*Joshua 4:21-24*

> *Hear this, you elders; give ear, all inhabitants of the land! Has such a thing happened in your days, or in the days of your fathers? Tell your children of it, and let your children tell their children, and their children to another generation.* —*Joel 1:2-3*

[Q] When have you been successful at teaching your children about God?

[Q] What are some of the best things God has done for your family?

Notes:

- Fathers need to be careful not to practice double standards (say one thing, but do another). Also, both parents need to be in agreement.
- Ensure that all teaching and admonition is clear to the child — that he or she understands.
- Be sure your teaching is biblical, and that you clearly understand why you believe it. Children will pick up on your doubt if it's there.

Another key to godly fathering is establishing house rules that are based on the truths found in God's Word.

> *Let the word of Christ dwell in you richly, teaching and admonishing one another in all wisdom, singing psalms and hymns and spiritual songs, with thankfulness in your hearts to God.*
> *—Colossians 3:16*

> *And let us consider how to stir up one another to love and good works. —Hebrews 10:24*

[Q] How does your family determine house rules?

[Q] How can you make sure your family's rules are based on God's Word?

DISCUSSING MENTORING

God calls us to be mentors to our children.

A mentor:

- A listens well
- Acts as a positive role model
- Seeks teachable moments
- Provides guidance and advice
- Offers encouragement and support

IMPORTANT TIPS FOR STEPFAMILIES

- To have a successful stepfamily, you must keep a high view of marriage — the relationship between husband and wife takes priority over children.
    - A child-centered home will always experience trouble because the children will eventually grow up and leave — this leaves you as a couple with a relationship in shambles.
    - Your commitment to any of your children is temporary; your commitment to your spouse is for a lifetime.
    - For children, your example of setting your spouse ahead of them is the model they need to see for their own future marriage (Ephesians 5:22-33).
    - The powerful and natural desire to love your own children must be surrendered to the higher priority of being a godly mate and loving spouse.
- Be responsible for your current family! Own your personal responsibility, regardless of bad behavior by others.
- Remember, the battle is in the heart and the mind.

Lesson 9

HOMEWORK

Complete the following assignments before the group gathers for Lesson 10.

Read Ephesians 4:29, then answer the following questions:

1. What three things should we consider before speaking?

2. How can this help you discipline your children?

3. How can you apply this verse to your life?

Look again at Ephesians 6:1-4, then answer the following questions:

1. What are the truths expressed in these verses?

2. What are the challenges and commands expressed in these verses?

3. How do these verses connect with Ephesians 4:29?

Review this week's memory verse:

Train up a child in the way he should go; even when he is old he will not depart from it.
—Proverbs 22:6

LESSON 10 **MEMORY VERSE**

Your word is a lamp to my feet and a light to my path.

—Psalm 119:105

Lesson 10

FATHERING (PART 3)

REVIEW

Remember the main purpose of our study: to provide an overview of what the Bible says about God, man, marriage and fathering.

Here are the key topics we covered during our last meeting:

- Children look up to their fathers.
- Children need discipline; their hearts are foolish when young.
- Godly families (including stepfamilies) have a high view of marriage where the relationship between husband and wife is the priority.

LESSON 10 OBJECTIVES

Here are the objectives for discussion this week:

- Define the general objective for godly training: to love God and love people.
- Learn how to use the Bible to teach children about sex.
- Read suggested verses for pride, drinking, honesty, money and anger.

GET TO KNOW GOD'S WORD

Opening question: Which self-help books have recently been popular in our society?

[Q] What do these books teach?

- We could fill entire libraries with all the books that have been published in order to answer the bigger questions about life and happiness. But that would be wasteful and unnecessary.
- That's because the Bible answers all of man's greatest questions, including:
  - Where did I come from?
  - What is my purpose?
- The Bible covers all areas of life, including:
  - Family and parenting
  - Anthropology, sociology, psychology
  - Government, labor, the church, science, language and history.

MAIN TOPIC – FATHERING (PART 3)

[Q] Are some parts of the Bible more important than others? Explain.

All parts of the Bible are equally inspired by God, but some verses and ideas are identified as more important than others.

> *And one of them, a lawyer, asked Him a question to test Him. "Teacher, which is the*

> *great commandment in the Law?" And He said to him, "You shall love the Lord your God with all your heart and with all your soul and with all your mind. This is the great and first commandment. And a second is like it: You shall love your neighbor as yourself. On these two commandments depend all the Law and the Prophets."* —Matthew 22:35-40

These verses help us understand our main goal as parents. We teach and discipline our kids in order to help them love God and others.

[Q] Why is this an important goal for us as fathers?

If we love God, we will obey Him. If we love other people, we will treat them like we want to be treated. This is what we hope to accomplish in the lives of our children.

Another important goal for fathering and godly discipline is to help our children realize that we all follow one of two paths. We either obey God each day or we disobey Him — and each path has consequences.

> *Blessed is the man who walks not in the counsel of the wicked, nor stands in the way of sinners, nor sits in the seat of scoffers; but his delight is in the law of the LORD, and on His law he meditates day and night. He is like a tree planted by streams of water that yields its fruit in its season, and its leaf does not wither. In all that he does, he prospers. The wicked are not so, but are like chaff that the wind drives away. Therefore the wicked will not stand in the judgment, nor sinners in the congregation of the righteous; for*

the LORD knows the way of the righteous, but the way of the wicked will perish. —Psalm 1:1-6

[Q] What do you like best about these verses? Why?

[Q] How do these verses help us understand the idea of two paths?

Finally, it's important for us to use godly discipline as parents because it helps our children understand the seriousness of sin — and that sin always brings consequences.

But each person is tempted when he is lured and enticed by his own desire. Then desire when it has conceived gives birth to sin, and sin when it is fully grown brings forth death. —James 1:14-15

The end of the matter; all has been heard. Fear God and keep His commandments, for this is the whole duty of man. For God will bring every deed into judgment, with every secret thing, whether good or evil. —Ecclesiastes 12:13-14

[Q] Why is it important for everyone to understand the seriousness of sin?

[Q] How can we teach our children about the consequences of sin?

But what comes out of the mouth proceeds from the heart, and this defiles a person. For out of the heart come evil thoughts, murder, adultery, sexual immorality, theft, false witness, slander. These are what defile a person.
—Matthew 15:18-20a

[Q] What do these verses teach about the source of sin?

REVIEW

[Q] What did you learn from this week's homework? What questions would you like to ask?

[Q] How has what you learned helped you understand God better?

[Q] How has what you learned helped you understand yourself better?

Recite the memory verse from Lesson 9:

> *Train up a child in the way he should go; even when he is old he will not depart from it.*
> *—Proverbs 22:6*

DISCUSSING THE BIBLE

[Q] What have you learned about the Bible during this lesson?

[Q] What are some steps you can take to learn more about God's Word?

DISCUSSING FATHERING

[Q] How would you summarize the main goals for fathering and godly discipline?

[Q] What emotions do you experience when you think about those goals? Why?

As parents, we don't have all the wisdom we need to teach our children about the bigger questions of life. Thankfully, we can rely on God's Word when it comes time for us to guide our children down the more complicated roads of life.

For example, the Bible helps us teach our children about sex in two main ways. First, we can help our children understand God's plan for sex and sexuality.

> *Therefore a man shall leave his father and his mother and hold fast to his wife, and they shall become one flesh. And the man and his wife were both naked and were not ashamed.*
> *—Genesis 2:24-25*

> *Let marriage be held in honor among all, and let the marriage bed be undefiled, for God will judge the sexually immoral and adulterous.*
> *—Hebrews 13:4*

[Q] How would you summarize God's plan for sex and sexuality?

Second, the Bible helps us understand the consequences of rebelling against God's plan for sex.

> *He who commits adultery lacks sense; he who does it destroys himself. He will get wounds and dishonor, and his disgrace will not be wiped away.*
> *—Proverbs 6:32-33*

> *Flee from sexual immorality. Every other sin a person commits is outside the body, but the sexually immoral person sins against his own body. Or do you not know that your body is a*

temple of the Holy Spirit within you, whom you have from God? You are not your own, for you were bought with a price. So glorify God in your body. —1 Corinthians 6:18-20

[Q] What are some of the consequences we receive when we go against God's plan for sex and sexuality?

[Q] How can you teach these consequences to your children?

The Bible also helps us teach about sex and consequences because it tells the story of several men and women who encountered God's plan in different ways. For example:

- Joseph's encounter with Potiphar's wife helps us understand how to deal with sexual temptation (Genesis 39:6-23).
- David's encounter with Bathsheba offers a negative example for dealing with temptation (2 Samuel 11:2-17).
- Psalm 51 is a great example of David's sorrow after giving in to temptation and committing sexual sin.

The Bible also helps us understand (and teach our children) how to avoid sin.

I have made a covenant with my eyes; how then could I gaze at a virgin? What would be my portion from God above and my heritage from the Almighty on high? Is not calamity for the unrighteous, and disaster for the workers of iniquity? Does not He see my ways and number all my steps? —Job 31:1-4

How can a young man keep his way pure? By guarding it according to Your word. With my whole heart I seek You; let me not wander from

Your commandments! I have stored up Your word in my heart, that I might not sin against You.
—Psalm 119:9-11

[Q] What do these verses teach about avoiding sin?

The Bible helps us teach and correct our children on several important topics. Here are some examples with suggested Scripture readings:

- **To teach about pride:** Proverbs 8:13, 11:2, 16:18, 18:12, 21:24, 27:1, 29:23; Daniel 4:4-37; 2 Samuel 24:1-25
- **To teach about drinking:** Proverbs 20:1, 23:19-21, 23:29-35; 1 Corinthians 5:11, 6:9-11; 1 Peter 4:1-4
- **To teach about honesty:** Exodus 20:16; Psalm 19:14; Proverbs 8:6-8, 12:22, 19:9; Ephesians 4:15, 4:25, 4:29
- **To teach about money:** Matthew 6:24; Romans 13:8; 1 Timothy 6:10
- **To teach about anger:** Proverbs 10:12, 12:16, 14:16-17, 15:1, 15:18, 19:11, 25:28, 29:22, 30:33; Matthew 5:21-22; Ephesians 4:26; Colossians 3:8; James 1:19-20

Lesson 10

HOMEWORK

Complete the following assignments before the group gathers for Lesson 11.

Read Daniel 4:4-37, then answer the following questions:

1. What's your initial reaction to these verses? Why?

2. How can you use these verses to teach children about pride?

3. What's the difference between healthy pride and sinful pride?

4. What are some ways to prevent sinful pride?

Read Exodus 20:1-20, then answer the following questions:

1. Which of these commandments did you struggle with as a child?

2. Which do you struggle with now?

3. How can you teach these commandments to your children?

Review this week's memory verse:

> *Your word is a lamp to my feet and a light to my path. —Psalm 119:105*

LESSON 11 **MEMORY VERSE**

*And He will turn the hearts
of fathers to their children
and the hearts of children
to their fathers ...*

—Malachi 4:6

Lesson 11

INMATE CHALLENGE

LESSON 10 REVIEW

Here are the key topics we covered during our last meeting:

- Highlight the basic goal of godly training: to love God and love people.
- How to use the Bible to teach children about sex and other issues.

LESSON 11 OBJECTIVES

Here are the key objectives for discussion this week:

- Explore what it means to live as a godly man while incarcerated.
- Explore what it looks like to be a godly spouse while in prison.
- Explore how to love and discipline children while incarcerated.

MAIN TOPIC – INMATE CHALLENGE

Watch the video from the *Inmate Challenge* DVD, produced by Awana Lifeline™.

This video is an unscripted, unedited response to this simple question: "If you could talk to other inmates across the country about being a godly man, a godly spouse, and a godly parent, what would you say?"

As you listen to the stories and the wisdom of the inmates featured in this video, use the following questions as a way of recording your reactions to what you see.

REACTIONS

Record your personal reactions as you watch the video.

[Q] What did you like best about the conversation between Ron, Darryl and George?

[Q] How is God speaking to you through their words?

[Q] Which of their ideas or suggestions can you apply in your life?

TEACHING CONTENT

Record some of the main principles taught by Ron, Darryl and George.

[Q] What have you learned about being a father?

[Q] What have you learned about being a provider for your family?

[Q] What have you learned about good and bad habits?

[Q] What have you learned about being a godly member of your extended family?

MORE ABOUT AWANA LIFELINE

Since 2004, Awana Lifeline has been working with prisons around the country to help inmate fathers understand and live out their responsibilities as fathers, despite being incarcerated.

Launched at Louisiana State Penitentiary at Angola, our work has now reached several dozen other prisons across the country, all with the goal of reaching our mission: to help men build a legacy of faith in Christ among their families.

REVIEW

[Q] What did you learn from this week's homework? What questions would you like to ask?

[Q] How has what you learned helped you understand God better?

[Q] How has what you learned helped you understand yourself better?

Review the memory verse from Lesson 10:

> *Your word is a lamp to my feet and a light to my path. —Psalm 119:105*

DISCUSSING THE INMATE CHALLENGE

[Q] What are your initial reactions from the video?

[Q] What emotions did you experience while you watched? Why?

> *For the eyes of the LORD run to and fro throughout the whole earth, to give strong support to those whose heart is blameless toward Him. —2 Chronicles 16:9*

George said: "When I read that, I knew at that moment that God wanted to use me. I knew that, in spite of everything that I've done and everything I did up until that moment, God wanted to use me."

[Q] Do you feel like God wants to use you?

[Q] Describe some of the main challenges you face in terms of being used by God in your current situation.

[Q] What are some opportunities for God to use you in your current situation?

Darryl said: "Children are going to emulate us; they're going to pattern their lives after us ... I know some who actually resent their fathers, but they ended up being just like their fathers — the same people they resent. So we have to have that strong relationship with God, because only through that relationship with

God are we going to be empowered to be a good example for our children."

[Q] Given your current situation, what do you fear most for your children? Why?

[Q] What do you want most for your children? Why?

George said: "We must see ourselves as assets … I don't see myself as a prisoner; I don't see myself as an inmate. I see myself as a son of the living God. I'm blessed. And because my family's connected to me, they're blessed."

> *But to all who did receive Him, who believed in His name, He gave the right to become children of God, who were born, not of blood nor of the will of the flesh nor of the will of man, but of God. —John 1:12-13*

[Q] Do you see yourself the way God sees you? Explain.

[Q] What does it mean to be children of God, in your experience?

Ron said: "There's not a person that's in prison that does not deal with loneliness … But I believe that God is able, in those moments, to give us His loving-kindness and to wrap His arms around us."

"The Bible says that in our weaknesses is when His strength is made perfect. We will never experience God's strength in our lives until we get to the place where we understand, 'I'm helpless!'"

> *But He said to me, "My grace is sufficient for you, for My power is made perfect in weakness."*

> *Therefore I will boast all the more gladly of my weaknesses, so that the power of Christ may rest upon me. For the sake of Christ, then, I am content with weaknesses, insults, hardships, persecutions, and calamities. For when I am weak, then I am strong.* —2 Corinthians 12:9-10

[Q] Do you find it easy or difficult to admit your weakness? Explain.

[Q] What does it look like to turn to God when we need help? How do we find Him?

Ron said: "I hear this a lot in prison … 'I'm going to wait till I get out to start going to church. I'm going to wait till I get out to start serving God. I'm going to wait till I get out to do this and that.' And guess what — it never happens when you get out. Why? Because you get consumed with what's going on in the world."

[Q] What decisions do you need to make while you're in prison?

[Q] What steps do you need to take while you're in prison?

[Q] What steps do you need to take right now?

HOMEWORK

Complete the following assignments before the group gathers for Lesson 12.

Take a moment to think deeply about the following questions, and to answer them honestly from your heart.

1. What kind of man do you want to be after you're finished with prison?

2. What kind of husband do you want to be after you're released from prison?

3. What kind of father do you want to be after you're released?

4. What kind of provider do you want to be once you are released?

5. Do you believe you can become the person you want to be? Explain.

6. How can you start becoming that person now? What steps do you need to take?

Review the verses you learned in the previous lessons.

Lesson 1:

> *In the beginning, God created the heavens and the earth. —Genesis 1:1*

Lesson 2:

> *Keep your heart with all vigilance, for from it flow the springs of life. —Proverbs 4:23*

Lesson 3:

> *For God so loved the world, that He gave His only Son, that whoever believes in Him should not perish but have eternal life. —John 3:16*

Lesson 4:

> *Sanctify them in the truth; Your word is truth. —John 17:17*

Lesson 5:

> *To each is given the manifestation of the Spirit for the common good. —I Corinthians 12:7*

Lesson 6:

> *Therefore a man shall leave his father and his mother and hold fast to his wife, and they shall become one flesh. —Genesis 2:24*

Lesson 7:

> *Husbands, love your wives, as Christ loved the church and gave Himself up for her.*
> *—Ephesians 5:25*

Lesson 8:

> *In the fear of the LORD one has strong confidence, and his children will have a refuge.*
> *—Proverbs 14:26*

Lesson 9:

> *Train up a child in the way he should go; even when he is old he will not depart from it.*
> *—Proverbs 22:6*

Lesson 10:

> *Your word is a lamp to my feet and a light to my path. —Psalm 119:105*

THE MALACHI DADS PLEDGE

As a Malachi Dad, I solemnly pledge to glorify God and build His kingdom by prioritizing the raising of godly children, first in my family, then in the influencing of other men to do the same in theirs. I firmly believe that my transformed life in Christ — my life of integrity, pursuit of this vision, and the pursuit of godly character — will allow me to impact my children, family, and others towards this end.

I will practice a life of daily discipline and dependence on God through prayer and the study of God's Word for the wisdom in how to "nurture my children in the admonition of the Lord." I will pursue this endeavor for a lifetime whether my children are in my home or not.

Finally, I believe that my end goal is not only for my children to walk in the Lord but this God-given vision would impact multiple generations to come.

So help me God.

Review this week's memory verse:

> *And He will turn the hearts of fathers to their children and the hearts of children to their fathers ... —Malachi 4:6*

LESSON 12 **MEMORY VERSE**

... Choose this day whom you will serve ... But as for me and my house, we will serve the LORD.

—Joshua 24:15

Lesson 12

THE HEART

REVIEW

Recite the Malachi Dads Pledge:

As a Malachi Dad, I solemnly pledge to glorify God and build His kingdom by prioritizing the raising of godly children, first in my family, then in the influencing of other men to do the same in theirs. I firmly believe that my transformed life in Christ — my life of integrity, pursuit of this vision, and the pursuit of godly character — will allow me to impact my children, family, and others towards this end.

I will practice a life of daily discipline and dependence on God through prayer and the study of God's Word for the wisdom in how to "nurture my children in the admonition of the Lord." I will pursue this endeavor for a lifetime whether my children are in my home or not.

Finally, I believe that my end goal is not only for my children to walk in the Lord but this God-given vision would impact multiple generations to come.

So help me God.

LESSON 12 OBJECTIVES

Here are the key objectives for discussion this week:

- Show the relationship between behavior and the heart — the inner man.
- Reinforce the importance of godly counsel, friends and choices.
- Demonstrate the consequences of choices.

MAIN TOPIC – THE HEART

[Q] Do you think it's easier to live as a Christian or a nonbeliever? Explain.

One of the things the Bible makes clear is that a life spent in rebellion against God is difficult and filled with trouble.

> *There is a way that seems right to a man, but its end is the way to death. —Proverbs 16:25*
>
> *Good sense wins favor, but the way of the treacherous is their ruin. —Proverbs 13:15*
>
> *For the one who sows to his own flesh will from the flesh reap corruption, but the one who sows to the Spirit will from the Spirit reap eternal life. —Galatians 6:8*

[Q] How have you experienced the difficult consequences of rebelling against God?

[Q] Where do you see evidence in our culture that choosing to walk away from God causes many problems?

When we choose to walk in submission to God, our lives become much simpler. This doesn't mean we won't ever have problems or that we'll always get what we want. Rather, it means that we will find peace even in difficult circumstances because we know God is in control.

> *Come to Me, all who labor and are heavy laden, and I will give you rest. Take My yoke upon you, and learn from Me, for I am gentle and lowly in heart, and you will find rest for your souls. For My yoke is easy, and My burden is light.*
> *—Matthew 11:28-30*

[Q] When have you felt like you were desperate for rest?

> *The thief comes only to steal and kill and destroy. I came that they may have life and have it abundantly. —John 10:10*

> *But the fruit of the Spirit is love, joy, peace, patience, kindness, goodness, faithfulness, gentleness, self-control; against such things there is no law. —Galatians 5:22-23*

[Q] How have you experienced the benefits of following God?

Because of sin, we're not able to follow God and obey His plans for our life under our own power. Instead, God transforms us from the inside out, giving us a new heart — a new inner self.

> *And I will give them one heart, and a new spirit I will put within them. I will remove the heart of stone from their flesh and give them a heart of flesh, that they may walk in My statutes and keep My rules and obey them. And they shall be My people, and I will be their God. —Ezekiel 11:19-20*

How do we know if God has given us a new heart and empowered us to follow Him? If we begin to demonstrate godly habits in our lives. Here are some practical thoughts on what it means to practice godly habits:

- Our primary goal in life should be to please God (2 Corinthians 5:9). This is the starting point for godly habits.
- We please God by acting more and more like Jesus Christ.
  - Matthew 3:17
  - Romans 8:28-29
- God knows we will never be perfect, but He wants us to grow through the power of the Holy Spirit.
  - Ephesians 4:22-24
  - 2 Peter 3:18

[Q] What habits would you like to develop as you continue living for God?

REVIEW

[Q] What are some words that describe the kind of man you want to become?

[Q] How will you take the first step in order to become that person?

Recite the memory verse from Lesson 11:

> *And He will turn the hearts of fathers to their children and the hearts of children to their fathers … —Malachi 4:6*

DISCUSSING THE HEART

Following God will lead us to many decision points where we must choose to obey what God wants us to do or take action based on our own desires. The choices we make when confronted with these decision points will reveal the condition of our hearts.

> *For the word of God is living and active, sharper than any two-edged sword, piercing to the division of soul and of spirit, of joints and of marrow, and discerning the thoughts and intentions of the heart. And no creature is hidden from His sight, but all are naked and exposed to the eyes of Him to whom we must give account. —Hebrews 4:12-13*

[Q] What's your initial reaction to these verses? Why?

There are several attitudes or "heart conditions" that God wants us to avoid if we are to follow Him. First, the Bible teaches us not to have a double-minded heart. This is the kind of heart that knows one thing to be true, but behaves in a way that goes against the truth.

> *Draw near to God, and He will draw near to you. Cleanse your hands, you sinners, and purify your hearts, you double-minded. —James 4:8*

> *Therefore you have no excuse, O man, every one of you who judges. For in passing judgment on another you condemn yourself, because you, the judge, practice the very same things. We know that the judgment of God rightly falls on those who practice such things. Do you suppose, O man*

— you who judge those who practice such things and yet do them yourself — that you will escape the judgment of God? —Romans 2:1-3

[Q] Why is it so easy for us to make choices in life that are hypocritical?

Second, God wants us to avoid hearts that are filled with bitterness. Bitterness is a foothold for resentment and the origin of anger. Therefore, a heart of bitterness not only affects the person who is bitter, but also the people around that person in a very destructive way.

When my soul was embittered, when I was pricked in heart, I was brutish and ignorant; I was like a beast toward You. —Psalm 73:21-22

See to it that no one fails to obtain the grace of God; that no "root of bitterness" springs up and causes trouble, and by it many become defiled. —Hebrews 12:15

[Q] What about your current situation makes it easy for bitterness to reside in your heart?

[Q] How can you fight against bitterness?

Third, God wants us to avoid pride in our hearts. Pride clouds our thinking and affects our behavior. To avoid pride, however, we must be humble.

Pride goes before destruction, and a haughty spirit before a fall. —Proverbs 16:18

For the wicked boasts of the desires of his soul, and the one greedy for gain curses and renounces the LORD. In the pride of his face the wicked does not seek Him; all his thoughts are, "There is no God." —Psalm 10:3-4

[Q] Describe the symptoms of a heart that is struggling with pride.

[Q] What are some ways to grow in humility as a follower of God?

So far we've looked at several characteristics and choices that God wants us to avoid. Now let's look at the kind of heart God wants us to develop as His Spirit changes us from the inside out.

First, God wants us to develop hearts that are clean. This means we must repent of our sins and ask forgiveness from God. God will do His part to create the clean heart, but we have to be willing to repent (turn from) from the sin that brought about the unclean condition in the first place.

Create in me a clean heart, O God, and renew a right spirit within me. —Psalm 51:10

[Q] Why is it that God must create a clean heart inside of us, instead of us choosing to clean ourselves?

[Q] What emotions do you experience when you think about the opportunity to have a clean heart? Why?

Second, God wants us to develop glad hearts as we live for Him. One part of the fruit of the Spirit is joy. Therefore, joy is evidence of the Spirit's work in a person's heart and life. People with a glad heart focus on three things: who God is (Psalm 104); what God has done (Psalm 107); and what God will do (Psalm 110).

Therefore my heart is glad, and my whole being rejoices; my flesh also dwells secure.—Psalm 16:9

Finally, God wants us to develop hearts that are steadfast as we follow Him. A steadfast heart doesn't quit; it doesn't give up, and it's not easily moved when the winds of trial and pressures come its way. That's because such hearts are focused on God's steadfast love (Psalm 107:43), faithfulness (Psalm 108:4), and God's deliverance and power (Psalm 108:13).

> *They set a net for my steps; my soul was bowed down. They dug a pit in my way, but they have fallen into it themselves. Selah. My heart is steadfast, O God, my heart is steadfast!*
> *—Psalm 57:6-7a*

> *My heart is steadfast, O God! I will sing and make melody with all my being! —Psalm 108:1*

[Q] Why is steadfastness an important quality for men who are incarcerated?

[Q] What obstacles get in the way of us developing the kinds of characteristics God desires?

[Q] How can these obstacles be overcome?

We've spent three months exploring what it means to be a man of God, including the characteristics of a godly husband and a godly father. Let's remember that in order to become the kind of people we want to be, we must rely on God's power to create a new heart within us.

THE MALACHI DADS PLEDGE

As a Malachi Dad, I solemnly pledge to glorify God and build His kingdom by prioritizing the raising of godly children, first in my family, then in the influencing of other men to do the same in theirs. I firmly believe that my transformed life in Christ — my life of integrity, pursuit of this vision, and the pursuit of godly character — will allow me to impact my children, family, and others towards this end.

I will practice a life of daily discipline and dependence on God through prayer and the study of God's Word for the wisdom in how to "nurture my children in the admonition of the Lord." I will pursue this endeavor for a lifetime whether my children are in my home or not.

Finally, I believe that my end goal is not only for my children to walk in the Lord but this God-given vision would impact multiple generations to come.

So help me God.

Name: ______________________ Date: 5/29/16

FACILITATOR NOTES

LARGE GROUP PLAN

Begin with an opening prayer.

Introduce the facilitators. Use first names only and remind participants that each facilitator is there to help them know God and learn how to live a life that honors God.

INTRODUCE THE PROGRAM

Begin the first lesson by briefly introducing the Malachi Dads program and goals. Use the following outline as a guide:

TIME	The group will meet for two hours each week over the next 12 weeks.
PURPOSE	Our goal is to provide an overview of what the Bible says about creation, God, men, marriage, and being a father.

FORMAT	We will start each meeting as one large group to introduce and teach the main topic, which will be different for each lesson. Then we will break into small groups in order to accomplish the following: · Discuss the topic in more detail. · Consider choices and consequences. · Review homework. · Pray.

SMALL GROUP DISCUSSION RULES

- One person talks at a time.
- No disrespectful comments. Only use positive, respectful language.
- Talk about yourself, not others.
- Make sure everyone gets a chance to talk.
- Stay focused.
- What people say in the group should stay in the group.

KEY BELIEFS

These are important truths that our group believes.

- God is real, and He is in charge of all things.
- God's Word is true. God gave us the Bible for our benefit and guidance.

- The Bible is all we need to understand our world, and to live in a way that pleases God. Following the Bible allows us to help our families, neighbors, and country.

KEY THEME

Our key theme for the entire study is "Two Paths."

- Every day we must choose between two paths. We will either obey God or disobey God. We will choose to honor God or honor ourselves.
- There are consequences to each path.
- Each week in our small groups we will talk about the different choices we're facing, and which path those choices will take us on.

KEY VERSE

Our key verse for the entire study is Joshua 24:15.

> *... Choose this day whom you will serve ... But as for me and my house, we will serve the LORD.*

LESSON 1 KEY OBJECTIVES

- *The Bible is our reliable guide for life, and is our only source for truth.*
- *God is the Creator and Ruler of all things.*
- *People are God's creations who are made in His image and made to worship Him.*

GET TO KNOW GOD'S WORD

Each week you'll help your group understand a little more about the Bible and its role in God's kingdom. To start, here are some facts to help your group members understand why the Bible is a reliable source for truth.

Opening question: What do you like best about the Bible? Why?

- *The Bible was written between 1500 B.C. and A.D. 100, and it is the world's best-selling book.*
- *The Bible is the best-preserved book from the ancient world. That means there are far more ancient copies of the Bible than of other books that most people believe to be reliable and true. For example:*
  - *There are only five ancient copies of Aristotle's writings.*
  - *There are only seven ancient copies of a book called* Tetralogies, *which was written by Plato.*
  - *There are only 10 ancient copies of a book called* Gallic Wars, *which was written by Julius Caesar.*
  - *But there are more than 24,000 ancient copies of books in the Bible.*

- *The Bible was given to us by God and has been preserved by God throughout the centuries.*
- *The Bible was recorded by men who were inspired by God to write the different books of the Old Testament and New Testament.*

LARGE GROUP PLAN

Discuss the two major topics from Lesson 1: God and People. Use the questions marked with the [Q] symbol on pages 7-9 to help your group members get involved in the lesson and apply what they learn to their own lives.

Ask for volunteers to read any Bible verses out loud. (Or read them out loud yourself if that works best.)

SMALL GROUP PLAN

Divide the large group into smaller groups of four to six people (depending on the number of facilitators available). *Using the questions marked with the [Q] symbol on pages 9-12, discuss the main topics of this week's lesson.*

Close the small-group discussion with a time of prayer.

LARGE GROUP PLAN

Begin with an opening prayer.

Remind group members of the Malachi Dads program goals, discussion rules, and key beliefs, key theme, and key verse from pages 14–15.

LESSON 2 OBJECTIVES

Here are the objecives you'll be discussing in Lesson 2:

- *Determine a definition for sin.*
- *Examine the cause and consequences of our sin.*
- *Identify Satan's strategy for attacking our weakness so that we will be ready when the attack comes.*

GET TO KNOW GOD'S WORD

Continue helping your group members explore the Bible by reviewing the following reasons why we can trust God's Word.

MAIN TOPIC – SIN

Use the questions on pages 17–20 to address the topic of sin according to God's Word. (Look for the [Q] symbol.) *These questions will help your group members get involved in the lesson and apply what they learn to their own lives.*

SMALL GROUP PLAN

Divide the large group into smaller groups of four to six people (depending on the number of facilitators available). *Use the questions marked with the [Q] symbol on page 20 to discuss the main topics from this week's lesson.*

Use the questions on pages 21–23 to go over the homework from Lesson 1. Then, recite the memory verse from Lesson 1 as a group:

> *In the beginning, God created the heavens and the earth. —Genesis 1:1.*

Read Genesis 3:6 and 1 John 2:15–16 and try to identify what they teach about the nature of temptation. If time allows, also consider reading Matthew 4:1–11.

[Q] What are some ways we experience these kinds of temptations today?

[Answer] Remember that Satan was an important part of Adam and Eve's decision to sin.

[Q] What do John 8:44 and 1 Peter 5:8–9 teach us about Satan?

[Answer] These verses teach that Satan can be resisted and defeated.

[Q] How is Satan different from God?

[Q] How do we see these consequences impacting the world today?

[Answer] Adam and Eve were given a choice: believe and obey God, or believe and obey Satan. They chose to believe Satan and disobey God. Their choice resulted in terrible consequences for all people — including death.

We are given the same choice every day. Will we believe and obey God, or will we believe and obey Satan?

Close the small-group discussion with a time of prayer.

LARGE GROUP PLAN

Begin with an opening prayer.

LESSON 3 KEY TOPICS

Here are the key topics for discussion this week:

- *All people sin, which means all people are disqualified from eternal life with God.*
- *God chose to pay the penalty for our sin.*
- *God offers salvation to all sinners.*

GET TO KNOW GOD'S WORD

Continue helping your group members explore the Bible by reviewing the list of facts on page 29 about how the Bible was created.

MAIN TOPIC – SALVATION

Use the questions on pages 30-32 to address the topic of salvation according to God's Word.

SMALL GROUP PLAN

Divide the large group into smaller groups of four to six people (depending on the number of facilitators available). *Use the material on pages 32-37 to discuss the main topics from this week's lesson.*

Recite the memory verse from Lesson 2:

> *Keep your heart with all vigilance, for from it flow the springs of life. —Proverbs 4:23*

Read the following verses out loud or ask for a volunteer.

> *Because, if you confess with your mouth that Jesus is Lord and believe in your heart that God raised Him from the dead, you will be saved. For with the heart one believes and is justified, and with the mouth one confesses and is saved. —Romans 10:9-10*

> *And they said, "Believe in the Lord Jesus, and you will be saved ..." —Acts 16:31*

Recite this week's memory verse:

> *For God so loved the world, that He gave His only Son, that whoever believes in Him should not perish but have eternal life. —John 3:16*

Close the small-group discussion with a time of prayer.

LARGE GROUP PLAN

Begin with an opening prayer.

LESSON 4 KEY TOPICS

Here are the key topics for discussion this week:

- *All people sin, which means all people are disqualified from eternal life with God.*
- *God chose to pay the penalty for our sin.*
- *God offers salvation to all sinners.*

GET TO KNOW GOD'S WORD

Continue helping your group members explore the Bible by reviewing the facts about the Bible and prophecy on page 42.

MAIN TOPIC – SANCTIFICATION

Use the questions on pages 42-44 to address the topic of sanctification according to God's Word.

SMALL GROUP PLAN

Divide the large group into smaller groups of four to six people (depending on the number of facilitators available). *Use the material on pages 45-47 to discuss the main topics from this week's lesson. Use the questions on page 44 to review the homework from Lesson 3.*

Recite the memory verse from Lesson 3:

> *For God so loved the world, that He gave His only Son, that whoever believes in Him should not perish but have eternal life. —John 3:16*

Review the verses you learned in the previous lessons.

Lesson 1:

> *In the beginning, God created the heavens and the earth. —Genesis 1:1*

Lesson 2:

> *Keep your heart with all vigilance, for from it flow the springs of life. —Proverbs 4:23*

Lesson 3:

> *For God so loved the world, that He gave His only Son, that whoever believes in Him should not perish but have eternal life. —John 3:16*

Recite this week's memory verse:

> *Sanctify them in the truth; Your word is truth. —John 17:17*

Close the small-group discussion with a time of prayer.

LARGE GROUP PLAN

Begin with an opening prayer.

LESSON 5 KEY TOPICS

Here are the key topics for discussion this week:

- *Christ is the head of the Church, which is the body of all believers.*
- *The Holy Spirit empowers and motivates believers.*
- *Sanctification is accomplished within believers.*
- *The Church witnesses about the glory and grace of God in this world.*

GET TO KNOW GOD'S WORD

Continue helping your group members explore the Bible by reviewing the facts about archaeology and God's Word on page 55.

MAIN TOPIC – THE CHURCH

Use the questions on pages 55-57 to address the topic of church according to God's Word.

SMALL GROUP PLAN

Divide the large group into smaller groups of four to six people (depending on the number of facilitators available). *Use the material on pages 57-62 to discuss the main topics from this week's lesson.*

Use the questions on pages 50–51 to review the homework from Lesson 4.

Recite the memory verse from Lesson 4:

> *Sanctify them in the truth; Your word is truth. —John 17:17*

Review the verses you learned in the previous lessons.

Lesson 1:

> *In the beginning, God created the heavens and the earth. —Genesis 1:1*

Lesson 2:

> *Keep your heart with all vigilance, for from it flow the springs of life. —Proverbs 4:23*

Lesson 3:

> *For God so loved the world, that He gave His only Son, that whoever believes in Him should not perish but have eternal life. —John 3:16*

Recite this week's memory verse:

> *To each is given the manifestation of the Spirit for the common good. —1 Corinthians 12:7*

Close the small-group discussion with a time of prayer.

LARGE GROUP PLAN

Begin with an opening prayer.

LESSON 6 OBJECTIVES

Here are the key objectives for discussion this week:

- *Identify the origin of marriage.*
- *Explore the problems sin caused for marriage.*
- *Understand the biblical reasons for marriage.*

GET TO KNOW GOD'S WORD

Continue helping your group members explore the Bible by reviewing the interesting facts on page 68.

MAIN TOPIC – MARRIAGE (PART 1)

Use the questions on pages 69-70 to begin addressing the topic of marriage according to God's Word.

THE MALACHI DADS PLEDGE

Recite the pledge together as a group:

As a Malachi Dad, I solemnly pledge to glorify God and build His kingdom by prioritizing the raising of godly children first in my family, then in the influencing of other men to do the same in theirs. I firmly believe that my transformed life in Christ — my life of integrity, pursuit of this vision, and the pursuit of godly character — will allow me to impact my children, family and others towards this end.

I will practice a life of daily discipline and dependence on God through prayer and the study of God's Word for the wisdom in how to "nurture my children in the admonition of the Lord." I will pursue this endeavor for a lifetime whether my children are in my home or not.

Finally, I believe that my end goal is not only for my children to walk in the Lord but this God-given vision would impact multiple generations to come.

So help me God.

SMALL GROUP PLAN

Divide the large group into smaller groups of four to six people (depending on the number of facilitators available). *Use the material on pages 71-75 to discuss the main topics from this week's lesson.*

REVIEW

Use the questions on page 64 to review the homework from Lesson 5.

Recite the memory verse from Lesson 5:

> *To each is given the manifestation of the Spirit for the common good. —1 Corinthians 12:7*

Recite this week's memory verse:

> *Therefore a man shall leave his father and his mother and hold fast to his wife, and they shall become one flesh. — Genesis 2:24*

Close the small-group discussion with a time of prayer.

LARGE GROUP PLAN

Begin with an opening prayer. Review the Malachi Dads Pledge.

LESSON 7 OBJECTIVES

Here are the objectives for discussion this week:

- *Explore what it means to be a godly husband.*
- *Review the husband's role in a godly marriage.*

GET TO KNOW GOD'S WORD

Continue helping your group members explore the Bible by reviewing the facts on page 81.

MAIN TOPIC – MARRIAGE (PART 2)

Use the questions on pages 82-84 to begin addressing the topic of marriage according to God's Word.

SMALL GROUP PLAN

Divide the large group into smaller groups of four to six people (depending on the number of facilitators available). *Use the material on pages 84-87 to discuss the main topics from this week's lesson.*

REVIEW

Use the questions on page 77 to go over the homework from Lesson 6.

Recite the memory verse from Lesson 6:

> *Therefore a man shall leave his father and his mother and hold fast to his wife, and they shall become one flesh. —Genesis 2:24*

Recite this week's memory verse:

> *Husbands, love your wives, as Christ loved the church and gave Himself up for her.*
> *—Ephesians 5:25*

Close the small-group discussion with a time of prayer.

LARGE GROUP PLAN

Begin with an opening prayer. Review the Malachi Dads Pledge.

LESSON 8 OBJECTIVES

Here are the key objectives for discussion this week:

- *Clarify the relationship between fathers and children.*
- *Identify the characteristics of a godly family environment.*
- *Explore a warning to fathers.*

GET TO KNOW GOD'S WORD

Continue helping your group members explore the Bible by reviewing the facts on page 93.

MAIN TOPIC – FATHERING (PART 1)

Use the questions on pages 94-95 to begin addressing the topic of fathering according to God's Word.

SMALL GROUP PLAN

Divide the large group into smaller groups of four to six people (depending on the number of facilitators available). *Discuss the main topics of this week's lesson using the material on pages 95-100.*

REVIEW

Use the questions on page 88 to go over the homework from Lesson 7.

Recite the memory verse from Lesson 7:

> *Husbands, love your wives, as Christ loved the church and gave Himself up for her. —Ephesians 5:25*

Recite this week's memory verse:

> *In the fear of the LORD one has strong confidence, and his children will have a refuge. —Proverbs 14:26*

Close the small-group discussion with a time of prayer.

LARGE GROUP PLAN

Begin with an opening prayer. Review the Malachi Dads Pledge.

LESSON 9 OBJECTIVES

Here are the objectives for discussion this week:

- *Define godly discipline.*
- *Consider how to apply godly discipline.*
- *Identify culturally unbiblical ways to raise children.*
- *Summarize biblical advice for stepfamilies.*

GET TO KNOW GOD'S WORD

Continue helping your group members explore the Bible by reviewing the facts on page 104.

MAIN TOPIC – FATHERING (PART 2)

Use the questions on pages 104–107 to continue exploring what it means to be a godly father.

SMALL GROUP PLAN

Divide the large group into smaller groups of four to six people (depending on the number of facilitators available). *Discuss the main topics of this week's lesson using the material on pages 107–110.*

REVIEW

Use the questions on page 101 to go over the homework from Lesson 8.

Recite the memory verse from Lesson 8:

> *In the fear of the LORD one has strong confidence, and his children will have a refuge.*
> *—Proverbs 14:26*

Recite this week's memory verse:

> *Train up a child in the way he should go; even when he is old he will not depart from it.*
> *—Proverbs 22:6*

Close the small-group discussion with a time of prayer.

LARGE GROUP PLAN

Begin with an opening prayer. Review the Malachi Dads Pledge.

LESSON 10 OBJECTIVES

Here are the objectives for discussion this week:

- *Define the general objective for godly training: to love God and love people.*
- *Learn how to use the Bible to teach children about sex.*
- *Read suggested verses for pride, drinking, honesty, money and anger.*

GET TO KNOW GOD'S WORD

Continue helping your group members explore the Bible by reviewing the facts on page 116.

MAIN TOPIC – FATHERING (PART 3)

Use the questions on pages 116-119 to continue exploring what it means to be a godly father.

SMALL GROUP PLAN

Divide the large group into smaller groups of four to six people (depending on the number of facilitators available). *Discuss the main topics of this week's lesson using the material on pages 119-122.*

REVIEW

Use the questions on page 112 to go over the homework from Lesson 9.

Recite the memory verse from Lesson 9:

> *Train up a child in the way he should go; even when he is old he will not depart from it. —Proverbs 22:6*

Recite this week's memory verse:

> *Your word is a lamp to my feet and a light to my path. —Psalm 119:105*

Close the small-group discussion with a time of prayer.

LARGE GROUP PLAN

Begin with an opening prayer. Review the Malachi Dads Pledge.

LESSON 11 OBJECTIVES

Here are the key objectives for discussion this week:

- *Explore what it means to live as a godly man while incarcerated.*
- *Explore what it looks like to be a godly spouse while in prison.*
- *Explore how to love and discipline children while incarcerated.*

MAIN TOPIC – INMATE CHALLENGE

For the large-group portion of this gathering, show the video portion of the Inmate Challenge *DVD, produced by Awana Lifeline™.*

Order the Inmate Challenge *DVD through your Awana® Lifeline Mentor.*

This video is an unscripted, unedited response to this simple question: "If you could talk to other inmates across the country about being a godly man, a godly spouse, and a godly parent, what would you say?"

Ask: As you listen to the stories and the wisdom of the inmates featured in this video, use the questions on pages 127-128 as a way of recording your reactions to what you see.

REACTIONS

Allow participants to record their personal reactions as they watch the video.

TEACHING CONTENT

Allow participants to record some of the main principles taught by Ron, Darryl and George.

Ask: What have you learned about being a father?

Ask: What have you learned about being a provider for your family?

Ask: What have you learned about good and bad habits?

Ask: What have you learned about being a godly member of your extended family?

MORE ABOUT AWANA LIFELINE

Since 2004, Awana Lifeline has been working with prisons around the country to help inmate fathers understand and live out their responsibilities as fathers, despite being incarcerated.

Launched at Louisiana State Penitentiary at Angola, our work has now reached several dozen other prisons across the country, all with the goal of reaching our mission: to help men build a legacy of faith in Christ among their families.

SMALL GROUP PLAN

Divide the large group into smaller groups of four to six people (depending on the number of facilitators available). *Discuss the main topics of this week's lesson using the material on pages 128–131.*

REVIEW

Use the questions on page 123 to go over the homework from Lesson 10.

Recite the memory verse from Lesson 10:

> *Your word is a lamp to my feet and a light to my path. —Psalm 119:105*

Recite this week's memory verse:

> *And He will turn the hearts of fathers to their children and the hearts of children to their fathers ... —Malachi 4:6*

Close the small-group discussion with a time of prayer.

LARGE GROUP PLAN

Begin with an opening prayer.

Remind participants of the main purpose of this study: to provide an overview of what the Bible says about God, man, marriage and parenting.

Review the Malachi Dads Pledge.

LESSON 12 OBJECTIVES

Here are the key objectives for discussion this week:

- *Show the relationship between behavior and the heart — the inner man.*
- *Reinforce the importance of godly counsel, friends and choices.*
- *Demonstrate the consequences of choices.*

MAIN TOPIC – THE HEART

Use the questions on pages 138–140 to address what God desires for our inner selves.

SMALL GROUP PLAN

Divide the large group into smaller groups of four to six people (depending on the number of facilitators available). *Discuss the main topics of this week's lesson using the material on pages 140–144.*

REVIEW

Use the questions on page 132 to go over the homework from Lesson 11.

Recite the memory verse from Lesson 11:

> *And He will turn the hearts of fathers to their children and the hearts of children to their fathers ... —Malachi 4:6*

Recite this week's memory verse:

> *... Choose this day whom you will serve ... But as for me and my house, we will serve the LORD. —Joshua 24:15*

Close the small-group discussion with a time of prayer.

NOTES

NOTES

Also from Awana Lifeline ...

Hannah's Gift — The Heart of a Mother

Modeled after the life of Hannah and her son as told in the first two chapters of 1 Samuel in the Old Testament, this curriculum offers mothers the opportunity to parent from a distance and give a legacy of faith to their children.

Item 95241

Hannah's Gift – Family Restoration

From the first Hannah's Gift book, incarcerated moms have established the importance of on-going activity in the lives of their children. Moms must now take steps to prepare themselves to build healthy family structures upon release. We want to use the prophet Jeremiah's words and warnings as signposts to lead us along the journey to healthy relationships.

Item 97472

Malachi Dads: The Heart of a Man, Part 1

The Heart of a Man, Part 1 is the second book in the Malachi Dads curriculum. This study focuses on how to become a man with a heart that pleases God, no matter what our past sins and failures, and no matter our physical appearance.

Item 97523

Malachi Dads: The Heart of a Man, Part 2

Heart of a Man, Part Two is the 3rd book of the Malachi Dad curriculum. This study will address how to develop your godly character and integrity in your walk with God as it relates for your family and community.

Item 97855

Also from Awana Lifeline ...

Inmate Challenge DVD

Receive a compelling challenge from some of the most broken men in our society — inmate fathers.

Filmed on location at the famed Angola Prison in Louisiana, three inmate fathers share their stories and their challenge to other inmates. This DVD is an ideal launching point for jail or prison ministry and for challenging fathers to consider the legacy they are leaving. Includes a five-week small group discussion guide. Order along with *Malachi Dads, The Heart of a Father* curriculum. Running time: 45 minutes. Includes a five-week small group discussion guide.

Item 83509

Order today!

EMAIL: awanalifeline@awana.org
PHONE: 888-944-4292
ONLINE: awanalifeline.org/products